MARRIAGE FROM A TO Z FOR "SINGLES" STUDY GUIDE

(Designed for small group discussions, individual time with God or preparation for marriage)

By Carolyn Tatem

FOREVER
publishing

FOREVER PUBLISHING

Marriage from A to Z for Singles Study Guide
Copyright©2015 by Carolyn Tatem

Requests for information should be addressed to: marriagefromatoz@gmail.com

All rights reserved. No part of this book may be reproduced, stored in a retrieval system, or transmitted in any form or by any means--electronic, mechanical, photocopy, recording, or any other--except for brief quotations in printed reviews, without the prior permission of the publisher.

First published by Forever Publishing 7/09/2015

Library of Congress Control Number: 2015910926

ISBN: 978-0-996-2851-2-4

Scripture taken from the New King James Version. Copyright 1979, 1980, 1982, by Thomas Nelson, Inc. Used by permission. All rights reserved.

Printed in the United States of America

ACKNOWLEDGEMENTS

Thank you to all the single ladies who helped to make ***Marriage from A to Z for Singles*** a reality! Georgina Agyekum, Sandie Brooks, Rhonda Henderson, LaWanda Hughes, Omiana Muller, Alicia Steele, Leah Thompson and Kristine Wallace.

TABLE OF CONTENTS

INTRODUCTION vi

CHAPTER ONE: THE **A** PRINCIPLES 1
    ACCEPTANCE 1
    ADMIT 3
    ANGER 5
    APPRECIATION 7
    ATTENTION 9
    ATTITUDE 11

CHAPTER TWO: THE **B** PRINCIPLES 13
    BALANCE 13
    BEARING 15
    BELIEVE 17
    BIBLE 19
    BOUNDARIES 21

CHAPTER THREE: THE **C** PRINCIPLES 23
    CARE 23
    CELEBRATE 25
    CLASSES 27
    COMMUNICATION 29
    COUCH TIME 31

CHAPTER FOUR: THE **D** PRINCIPLES 33
    DATING 33
    DEVOTIONS 35
    DISCIPLINE 37
    DIVORCE 39

CHAPTER FIVE: THE **E** PRINCIPLES 41
    EATING 41
    ENCOURAGE 43
    ENDURE 45
    ENTERTAINING 47

CHAPTER SIX: THE **F** PRINCIPLES 49
    FAITHFUL 49
    FINANCES 51
    FORGIVENESS 53
    FRIENDSHIP 55

CHAPTER SEVEN: THE **G** PRINCIPLES 57
    GIVE 57
    GOALS 59
    GOD 61
    GODLY SEEDS 63

CHAPTER EIGHT: THE **H** PRINCIPLES 65
    HEALTH 65
    HELPER 67
    HONEY 69
    HOUSEWORK 71

CHAPTER NINE: THE **I** PRINCIPLES 73
    IN TUNE 73
    INITIATE 75
    INTIMACY 77
    ISOLATION 79

CHAPTER TEN: THE **J** PRINCIPLES 81
    JESUS 81
    JOINT ACCOUNTS 83
    JOY 85

CHAPTER ELEVEN: THE **K** PRINCIPLES 87
    KEEPING IT TOGETHER 87
    KINDNESS 89
    KING 91
    KISSING 93

CHAPTER TWELVE: THE **L** PRINCIPLES 95
    LEAVE AND CLEAVE 95
    LOVE 97

CHAPTER THIRTEEN: THE **M** PRINCIPLES 99
    MANAGE 99
    MANNERS 101
    MIRROR 103
    MULTIPLY 105

CHAPTER FOURTEEN: THE **N** PRINCIPLES 107
    NAGGING 107
    NEGATIVE 109
    NOTICE 111
    NOURISH 113

CHAPTER FIFTEEN: THE **O** PRINCIPLES 115
    OBEDIENCE 115
    ON TIME 117
    OPEN 119
    OPEN DOORS 121

CHAPTER SIXTEEN: THE **P** PRINCIPLES 123
    PARENTS 123
    PHONE CALLS 125
    PHOTOS 127
    PRAYER 129

CHAPTER SEVENTEEN: THE **Q** PRINCIPLES 131
    QUARRELS 131
    QUEEN 133
    QUIET 135
    QUIT 137

CHAPTER EIGHTEEN: THE **R** PRINCIPLES 139
    RECONCILIATION 139
    RELATIONSHIPS 141
    RESPECT 143

CHAPTER NINETEEN: THE **S** PRINCIPLES 145
    SEASONS 145
    SERVING 147
    SEX 149
    SUBMISSION 151

CHAPTER TWENTY: THE **T** PRINCIPLES 153
    TEMPTATION 153
    TIME 155
    TITHE 157
    TRUST 159

CHAPTER TWENTY-ONE: THE **U** PRINCIPLES 161
    UNDERSTANDING 161
    UNGODLY 163
    UNITY 165
    UPLIFT 167

CHAPTER TWENTY-TWO: THE **V** PRINCIPLES 169
    VACATION 169
    VALIDATE 171
    VARIETY 173
    VOWS 175

CHAPTER TWENTY-THREE: THE **W** PRINCIPLES 177
    WAIT 177
    WEDDING RING 179
    WITHHOLD 181
    WORDS 183
    WORRY 185

CHAPTER TWENTY-FOUR: THE **X**, **Y**, AND **Z** PRINCIPLES 187
    X-RAY 187
    YOU 189
    ZEBRA 191

PERSONAL REFLECTIONS 193

REFERENCES 194

INTRODUCTION

Are you single with a desire to get married? Maybe there is no one in the picture, but you are believing God for your husband or your wife. God is able! However, while you are waiting, you can prepare by becoming a better you and ultimately becoming a great wife or a great husband.

The ***Marriage from A to Z for Singles Study Guide*** was designed to be used with the book, ***Marriage from A to Z: Principles for a Successful Marriage***. However, this book is especially for singles who want to prepare themselves for marriage or simply become a better single. Don't wait until you meet Mr. or Ms. Right to become a good husband or wife. Become a better you or a good spouse beforehand.

This guide encourages the reader to think about each of the ***Marriage from A to Z*** principles. Each principle is based on the Word of God. There are four sections for each principle: **1)** Discussion Questions; **2)** A Look in the Word section which provides scripture that supports the principle; **3)** An Application section which gives a few tips on how one might apply the principles; and **4)** A Journal area to write thoughts about the principle. In addition, some principles include Extra Activities that may help to give further insight. This study guide would be great for a group discussion, pre-marital couples or as an individual study.

It is my prayer that God will use this study to bless every person who has a desire to prepare for marriage God's way.

CHAPTER ONE
THE A PRINCIPLES

ACCEPTANCE

DEFINITION: To take or receive with approval. (Accept yourself and others)

DISCUSSION QUESTIONS:

1. "What you see is what you get!" What do others see when they meet you?

2. What do you really like or admire about yourself? If applicable, what do you really like or admire about your potential spouse?

3. Is there anything that you don't like about yourself or your potential spouse? Examine how you respond to the dislikes.

4. When we don't accept, we tend to reject. What makes you feel accepted? What makes you feel rejected?

LOOK IN THE WORD:

1. Read Romans 15:7. What does this verse ask us to do?

2. Do you think God is pleased with the way you love yourself and others?

3. How can you better express love and acceptance towards yourself and others?

_____
_____
_____

APPLICATION:

1. Pray and ask God to help you totally accept yourself. If you have a potential spouse, ask God to help you totally accept him or her. Remember, no one is perfect.

2. Reflect on what makes you feel accepted or rejected. Identify scriptures that speak God's truth about how He created you and your identity in Him. Be more intentional about meditating on these verses.

_____
_____
_____

JOURNAL:

How did God speak to you about this principle? Is there anything you need to change? What do you need to continue?

_____
_____
_____
_____
_____
_____
_____
_____
_____
_____
_____
_____
_____
_____
_____
_____
_____
_____
_____

ADMIT

DEFINITION: To confess or acknowledge.

DISCUSSION QUESTIONS:

1. When you are wrong, do you normally admit it? Why or why not?

   _____
   _____
   _____

2. Why do you think people have problems with admitting their wrongs?

   _____
   _____
   _____

3. How do you respond when someone says, "I was wrong; will you forgive me?"

   _____
   _____
   _____

LOOK IN THE WORD:

1. Read II Kings 18:14. In this verse, the king was admitting that he was wrong. What did he say?

   _____
   _____
   _____

2. Why is it important for us to admit we are wrong?

   _____
   _____
   _____

APPLICATION:

1. Confess your wrongs to the Lord and ask God to forgive you.
2. When you realize that you are wrong, say I was wrong for _____. Will you forgive me?
3. Be willing to forgive when others admit to a wrong.
4. Always remember the grace and the mercy that God gives to you.

JOURNAL:

Oftentimes before healing, closure or deliverance can take place, one must be willing to ADMIT or verbalize their wrong. What do you think about this statement?

_____
_____
_____
_____
_____
_____
_____
_____
_____
_____
_____
_____
_____
_____
_____
_____
_____
_____
_____
_____

ANGER

DEFINITION: To become angry, painfully inflamed. Enrage, inflame to steam up, and tick off, outrage or madden.

DISCUSSION QUESTIONS:

1. Examine yourself. How do you normally deal with anger?

2. How do those closest to you deal with anger?

3. What is your normal reaction after something or someone has made you angry (raising your voice, slamming the door, silent treatment or showing outward signs of anger)?

4. Do you think that God is pleased with the way you express your anger?

LOOK IN THE WORD:

1. Read Ephesians 4:26. What instructions does this verse give on anger?

2. Give examples of how anger can lead you to sin.

3. When should we handle or deal with our anger?

APPLICATION:

1. Pray about the way that you and those closest to you express anger.
2. Watch your attitude and actions after you get angry.
3. If anger is really an issue for you, read I Corinthians 13 every day for 30 days. Ask God to speak to you about your anger.

JOURNAL:

What makes you angry the most? Give your anger to God. Write a prayer to God about your anger. If anger is not your issue, pray for someone who struggles with anger.

APPRECIATION

DEFINITION: Gratitude and thankful recognition.

DISCUSSION QUESTIONS:

1. When was the last time you said, "thank you" or "I appreciate you" to someone close to you?

2. How do you feel when those closest to you say thank you or express genuine appreciation?

3. What can you do today to show appreciation or express gratitude towards someone close to you?

4. List 3 things that you appreciate about someone close to you.

LOOK IN THE WORD:

1. Read Ephesians 6:6-8. What do these verses tell us about serving?

2. Read Psalm 92:1. What does this verse say about giving thanks to the Lord? How can you apply this to your relationships in general?

APPLICATION:

1. Serve from the heart.
2. Express genuine thanks and appreciation.
3. Notice the small things.
4. Don't take others for granted.
5. Practice thanking God and others on a regular basis.

EXTRA ACTIVITY:

1. Purchase or make a card of appreciation. Thank others for whatever God places on your heart.
2. Look for creative ways to say thank you. Make it a habit.

JOURNAL:

Write a letter of appreciation to the Lord for all He has done and is doing in your life.

_____
_____
_____
_____
_____
_____
_____
_____
_____
_____
_____
_____
_____
_____
_____
_____
_____
_____
_____

ATTENTION

DEFINITION: The act of applying the mind to something.

DISCUSSION QUESTIONS:

1. What does it mean to pay attention to others?

2. Pretend you are asked to give a description of a co-worker or a family member based on their appearance yesterday. Give as many details as possible from head to toe, include what you observed about their clothing, countenance, etc.

3. What did you notice about this co-worker or family member yesterday?

LOOK IN THE WORD:

1. Read Proverbs 4:1. We are encouraged to listen to instruction and pay attention. What do you gain when you pay attention?

3. How can this apply to paying attention to others?

APPLICATION:

1. Make time for others on a regular basis.
2. Compliment others on something that you have noticed.
3. Acknowledge others when leaving or entering an environment.
4. Pray and ask God to show you areas in your life where you may need to pay more attention.
5. Pay attention to the things that God has done recently.

JOURNAL:

How are you doing with paying attention to others? What are your thoughts about applying this principle to your relationships in general?

ATTITUDE

DEFINITION:

A feeling or emotion towards a fact or state.

DISCUSSION QUESTIONS:

1. List some benefits of having a positive attitude.

2. What is your attitude about being single?

3. What is your attitude about becoming a husband or a wife?

4. What is God's attitude towards marriage?

LOOK IN THE WORD:

1. Read Proverbs 118:21. What impact would you say that your tongue can have on a marriage/spouse?

2. What does attitude have to do with this verse?

APPLICATION:

1. Ask God to change your heart about any attitudes that do not please Him.
2. Read positive books about any attitudes that you need to change.
3. Write down a positive statement about your attitude towards any area of your life.

_____

_____

_____

JOURNAL:

Write about a situation where your attitude truly determined your altitude.

CHAPTER TWO
THE B PRINCIPLES

BALANCE

DEFINITION: A means of judging or deciding.

DISCUSSION QUESTIONS:

1. Are you doing a good job of balancing your time? (God, you, work, church, family, friends, etc.)

2. What are your priorities? Make a list of the things that require most of your time.

3. Where would you like to spend more time? Less time?

4. How do you determine what you will do first, second and third?

LOOK IN THE WORD:

1. Read Matthew 6:33. What does this scripture ask you to do? What does "seeking God first" mean to you?

2. What are the blessings of putting God first?

3. How can applying this verse make a difference in your schedule?

APPLICATION:
1. Examine your current schedule. Is there anything that needs to change?
2. Practice seeking God first. Begin each day with prayer and read something from God's Word.

JOURNAL:

If you could spend the day any way that you would like, how would you spend your time? Would the way you spend your time reflect what is important to you?

BEARING

DEFINITION: To be patient, forbearing. To endure and face hardship.

DISCUSSION QUESTIONS:

1. What is one of the most challenging things you have experienced in your lifetime?

2. Explain how you made it through the challenge. What is a lesson you learned as a result of the challenge?

3. What were some of your thoughts or emotions at the time of your challenge? Did you know the challenge would work out?

4. What would have happened if you would have quit or not continued during the challenge? Did the challenge involve or impact other people? How would they have been affected if you would have given up?

LOOK IN THE WORD:

1. Read I Corinthians 13:7. This scripture tells us that love _____ all things. What does it mean to bear ALL things?
2. Read Colossians 3:12 & 13. What does this scripture say about bearing?

APPLICATION:

1. Make a list of challenges you have now. Submit each challenge to the Lord in prayer. Ask God to help you to walk in His love.
2. Remember, love bears all things and God's grace is sufficient for you. He will give you the supernatural strength to bear ALL things.
3. When you are in the midst of a challenge, increase your prayer and Bible reading time. You will find strength like never before.

JOURNAL:

Thank you, Lord, for bearing the cross just for me. Teach me how to do what I Corinthians 13:7 says. Write a prayer to the Lord in reference to "Bearing ALL things."

_____
_____
_____
_____
_____
_____
_____
_____
_____
_____
_____
_____
_____
_____
_____
_____
_____
_____
_____
_____

BELIEVE

DEFINITION: To have confidence in the truth, the existence, or the reliability of something.

DISCUSSION QUESTIONS:

1. What are you believing God for right now? List at least two things.

   _____
   _____
   _____

2. How can unbelief impact your relationship with Him?

   _____
   _____
   _____

3. What is something that you have been believing since childhood?

   _____
   _____
   _____

LOOK IN THE WORD:

1. Read Mark 9:23. What does Jesus say about a person who believes?

   _____
   _____
   _____

2. What are the consequences of unbelief?

   _____
   _____
   _____

APPLICATION:

1. Find a scripture in reference to whatever you are believing God for. Write the scripture. Pray this scripture every time you think about what you are believing God for.

2. Don't be afraid to dream. Discuss a dream with a close friend.

JOURNAL:

Write a dream that you would like to see come true. Explain why you would like the dream to become a reality. "Only if one believes in something can one act purposefully" (dictionary.com).

BIBLE

DEFINITION: The Word of God.

DISCUSSION QUESTIONS:

1. Is reading the Bible a priority for you? How often do you currently read the Bible?

2. Why is reading the Bible (on a daily basis) very important?

3. What struggles might a person have with reading the Bible each day?

4. How might you benefit from daily Bible reading?

LOOK IN THE WORD:

1. Read Hosea 4:6. Why are God's people being destroyed?

2. Where can we get knowledge?

3. Think about something in your life that could have been better had you known better.

APPLICATION:

1. Find a quiet place to sit, pray (ask God to help you to understand His Word), open your Bible and read for 5 minutes. Read the Proverb of the day. So if today is the 25th, read Proverbs chapter 25.

2. Make reading the Word of God a priority for each day. Get a note pad and record what you read each day.

3. Be intentional about applying what you learn to your life and your potential marriage.

EXTRA ACTIVITY:

1. People often feel they don't have time to read God's Word. Here's an activity that demonstrates how efficient this process can be. You can do this with a group or family members. Provide each person with a page out of a devotional book or a passage of scripture. Set a timer for 3 minutes and ask them to read. Have them share and discuss what they have read. Emphasize the fact that it really doesn't take long to read something from God's Word. Encourage everyone to read the Bible every day.

JOURNAL:

The Bible is known as "Basic Instructions Before Leaving the Earth." What instructions have you received from reading the Word of God? How are you doing with following the instructions?

_____
_____
_____
_____
_____
_____
_____
_____
_____
_____
_____
_____
_____
_____
_____
_____
_____
_____

BOUNDARIES

DEFINITION: Something that indicates bounds or limits.

DISCUSSION QUESTIONS:

1. After reading the chapter on boundaries, what do you think about setting boundaries?

   _____
   _____
   _____

2. Why is it important to have boundaries in your life?

   _____
   _____
   _____

3. Have you established any boundaries in your relationships? List two boundaries.

   _____
   _____
   _____

LOOK IN THE WORD:

1. Read Ephesians 4:27. How does this verse relate to setting boundaries in a relationship?

   _____
   _____
   _____

2. How can a lack of boundaries be interpreted as making room for the devil?

   _____
   _____
   _____

APPLICATION:

1. Determine boundaries that you are willing to live by.
2. Discuss your boundaries with someone who will hold you accountable.
3. Do everything you can to honor the boundaries you have established.

JOURNAL:

Think about the boundaries that were established for you as a child. Although you may not have liked or understood them, write why they were necessary.

CHAPTER THREE
THE C PRINCIPLES

CARE

DEFINITION: Attending to someone or something.

DISCUSSION QUESTIONS:

1. Do your family and friends know that you care? List some of the things you do to show that you care.

2. What can others do to make you feel they care for you?

3. What expectations do you have for a spouse who wants to show that he or she cares?

LOOK IN THE WORD:

1. Read I Peter 5:7. What does this verse tell you to do?

2. What are some of the ways God demonstrates His care for you?

APPLICATION:

1. Make a list of all of the things that are cares and concerns for you. Pray about them.
2. Recognize that God cares for you. Therefore, we must be intentional about caring for others.
3. Discuss the things that you deeply care about with a close friend or your potential spouse. See if you care about the same things.

JOURNAL:

Think about the person who demonstrated care for you as a child. Write about the way they cared.

When I was a child, I remember _____ demonstrating their care for me by _____.

_____
_____
_____
_____
_____
_____
_____
_____
_____
_____
_____
_____
_____
_____
_____
_____
_____
_____

CELEBRATE

DEFINITION: To observe (a day) or commemorate (an event) with ceremonies or festivities.

DISCUSSION QUESTIONS:

1. When was the last time you celebrated a special event (for yourself or someone else)?

2. List days that are special to you and that you enjoy celebrating.

3. What is your idea of a true celebration? What do you like to do?

LOOK IN THE WORD:

1. Read Esther 9:18-29. How did the Jews celebrate their special days?

2. How often did they celebrate?

APPLICATION:

1. Pick a day and celebrate something special.
2. With little or no money, find a creative way to celebrate a special day or event (birthday, anniversary, the first day of something, or the last day of something). If you can't think of anything, celebrate the goodness of the Lord.
3. Be intentional about looking for days and events to celebrate; invite friends and family to help you celebrate.
4. Take pictures and create memories of the event.

JOURNAL:

If you could celebrate a special day or event any way that you would like and money was not an issue, what day would you celebrate? Write the details of your celebration below (the location, number of people, food, etc.).

_____
_____
_____
_____
_____
_____
_____
_____
_____
_____
_____
_____
_____
_____
_____
_____

CLASSES

DEFINITION: A group of students meeting regularly to study a subject under the guidance of a teacher.

DISCUSSION QUESTIONS:

1. Have you recently taken any classes to learn or help enhance yourself? (e. g., exercise, spiritual, educational, financial, etc.) If not, are you willing to take a class?

   _____
   _____
   _____

2. What are the benefits of taking a class?

   _____
   _____
   _____

3. If you could take any class with your potential spouse, what would it be?

   _____
   _____
   _____

LOOK IN THE WORD:

1. In Hosea 4:6 the scripture says that my people are destroyed for a lack of knowledge. How can this scripture relate to taking classes?

   _____
   _____
   _____

2. How can this scripture apply to being in a relationship?

   _____
   _____
   _____

APPLICATION:

1. Find a class in an area of interest to you. Register for the class.
2. If you can't commit to a long class, find a one day class or conference.
3. Be intentional about taking classes or attending a session that could help strengthen you in some way.

JOURNAL:

Think about a class, workshop or seminar you may have taken in the past. What did you learn from taking the class? Why is gaining knowledge and information so important?

COMMUNICATION

DEFINITION: To impart knowledge of, to make known, to transmit, to give or interchange thoughts and information.

DISCUSSION QUESTIONS:

1. On a scale of 1 to 10 (10 representing the greatest), how would you rate your ability to communicate effectively?

   _____
   _____
   _____

2. What could you do to improve your communication style?

   _____
   _____
   _____

3. Which way do you prefer to communicate: in person, by phone, text or email?

   _____
   _____
   _____

4. Are those in authority over you (supervisor, manager, etc.), pleased with the way (tone, attitude, level of respect) that you speak to him or her?

   _____
   _____
   _____

LOOK IN THE WORD:

1. Read Ephesians 4:29. What does this verse tell us to do and not to?

   _____
   _____
   _____

2. How can this verse apply to being in a relationship?

   _____
   _____
   _____

APPLICATION:

1. Think about the things that your family, friends or co-workers do well. Give a compliment to them by expressing it in words, with a card or writing a note.

2. Strive to do more listening to the people around you. Listen before you speak.

3. Evaluate your words. Do you tend to speak negatively or positively?

4. Pray and ask God to sharpen your communication skills with others.

JOURNAL

A lack of communication is a popular problem in relationships. What do you think are some of the obstacles that contribute to this problem? What can you do to improve your communication with others?:

___
___
___
___
___
___
___
___
___
___
___
___
___
___
___

COUCH TIME

DEFINITION: Taking time out of your day to sit on the couch next to each other to connect and communicate.

DISCUSSION QUESTIONS:

1. What do you think about the *Couch Time Principle*? The author mentions two ways to use this principle. What are they?

   _____
   _____
   _____

2. How often do you make time to sit down to bond with those to whom you are close?

   _____
   _____
   _____

3. How can sitting on the couch and spending quality time with those you love be beneficial?

   _____
   _____
   _____

4. When would be a good time for you to sit down and connect with those closest to you?

   _____
   _____
   _____

LOOK IN THE WORD:

1. Sitting on the couch requires being still. Read Psalm 46:10. What does this verse tell you to do? Be _____ and know that I am God. When we are still with a reverent heart, we learn more about Him and His ways.

2, How can you apply this same principle to your life?

   _____
   _____
   _____

APPLICATION:

1. Make "Couch Time" a regular practice in your relationships.
2. Start with 10 minutes. Use the time to catch up, laugh and encourage one another.
3. Enjoy being in the presence of those you love.

JOURNAL:

If possible, take a few minutes to sit on the couch. Imagine Jesus is sitting next to you. Write out your conversation with the Lord. Tell Jesus about your day, your concerns and your desires.

_____
_____
_____
_____
_____
_____
_____
_____
_____
_____
_____
_____
_____
_____
_____

CHAPTER FOUR
THE D PRINCIPLES

DATING

DEFINITION: To go out socially.

DISCUSSION QUESTIONS:

1. When was the last time that you had a date with God?

   _____
   _____
   _____

2. How often do you date God? (private time together, just the two of you)

   _____
   _____
   _____

3. Is having a date with God a priority? If not, what prevents you from having a date on a regular basis?

   _____
   _____
   _____

4. What is the difference between dating and courting?

   _____
   _____
   _____

LOOK IN THE WORD:

1. Read Proverbs 5:18. This verse says "rejoice with the wife of your youth." To rejoice is to be glad or to take delight in your wife.

   _____
   _____
   _____

2. How can you apply this scripture to the concept of dating God?

   _____
   _____
   _____

APPLICATION:

1. Develop a list of things that you would like to do and places that you would like to go.
2. Make a date to accomplish the things that are on your list. Invite a friend to join you.
3. Make it a goal to date the Lord on a regular basis.

JOURNAL:

If money and time were not an issue, describe your dream date. Write about where you would go, what you would do and what you might like to see.

_____
_____
_____
_____
_____
_____
_____
_____
_____
_____
_____
_____
_____
_____
_____

DEVOTIONS

DEFINITION: Profound dedication, earnest attachment to a cause or a person.

DISCUSSION QUESTIONS:

1. Are you devoted to spending time with the Lord? Why or why not?

2. Based on the *Devotions Principle* (page 24), what are some of the benefits of having devotional time with the Lord?

3. Why do you think we are so quick to devote time to everything else, but hesitate to devote time to the Lord?

LOOK IN THE WORD:

1. Read Matthew 18:20. What does this scripture tell us about coming together with others to spend time with the Lord?

2. Psalm 73:28 says it is good for me to draw near to God. How does praying and reading the Bible draw us near to God?

APPLICATION:

1. Commit a set time (morning, noon or night) to the Lord each day.
2. Pray and read the Word of God.
3. Try using a devotional book. (A book that focuses on the Lord).
I4. If you have children, incorporate having devotional time with them.

JOURNAL:

How is God speaking to you about your devotional time to Him? Have you been consistent, is it good or can it stand to be changed?

_____
_____
_____
_____
_____
_____
_____
_____
_____
_____
_____
_____
_____
_____
_____

DISCIPLINE

DEFINITION: Training to act in accordance with rules, instruction and exercise designed to train to proper conduct or action.

DISCUSSION QUESTIONS:

1. Is there anything that you would like to change about yourself?

2. What disciplines would you need to establish in order to see change?

3. What is something you do well that requires discipline?

LOOK IN THE WORD:

1. Read I Corinthians 9:27. What does it mean to discipline the body?

2. Is disciplining your body a challenge? Pray and ask God to help you in this area.

APPLICATION:

1. Think of 1-2 things that you really would like to accomplish. Write them down and ask God for the discipline that is necessary to accomplish this goal.
2. Commit to doing what it takes. Be consistent.
3. Ask someone to hold you accountable. Check in on a regular basis.

JOURNAL:

What changes do you think God would like for you to make? Write about the discipline necessary for the change to occur.

DIVORCE

DEFINITION: To break the marriage contract between oneself and one's spouse.

DISCUSSION QUESTIONS:

1. Have you or anyone that you know ever experienced a divorce? What were some of the challenges that you experienced or observed?

2. How does a divorce impact family, children and friends?

3. Define covenant. Compare how God views divorce versus how the world views divorce.

LOOK IN THE WORD:

1. Read Malachi 2:16b. What does God's word say about divorce?

2. What do you think violence and divorce have in common?

APPLICATION:

1. If you are considering marriage, remember that divorce should not be an option.
2. Seek godly counseling prior to getting married in order to receive a full understanding of the benefits and challenges involved in marriage.
3. Consult with people who have been married for 30, 40, or 50 years plus. Determine how they managed to never give up.

JOURNAL:

What are your thoughts on divorce? How is God speaking to you about divorce?

CHAPTER FIVE
THE E PRINCIPLES

EATING

DEFINITION: To consume food/meals specifically, at the table.

DISCUSSION QUESTIONS:

1. Do you eat meals at the table with your family and friends? Why or why not?

2. Do you cook your meals? Why or why not?

3. Based on the *Eating Principle*, how do you think your family or friends would benefit from eating together at the table?

LOOK IN THE WORD:

1. Read Exodus 25:8-9, 23-30. What was the purpose of the table?

2. How does God want to be included in your meals? "Jesus wants to meet you at the table." What does this mean to you?

APPLICATION:

1. If necessary, do something different to make your table more inviting. Add color, candles, placemats, a tablecloth or colored dishes.
2. Invite guests to your table.
3. Prepare meals that are good and healthy.

JOURNAL:

What are your thoughts about eating meals with friends and family? How can practicing this principle benefit the relationships in your family?

ENCOURAGE

DEFINITION: To inspire with courage, spirit, or confidence.

DISCUSSION QUESTIONS:

1. Think about something you would not have accomplished without encouragement.

2. What are the benefits of having someone to encourage you?

3. What could you say or do to encourage your family and friends in an area that they may need encouragement?

LOOK IN THE WORD:

1. Read Philippians 4:13. How can you use this scripture to encourage your friends, co-workers, family or others?

2. Based on this scripture, what is the key to accomplishing a task?

APPLICATION:

1. Be intentional about encouraging your family, friends and others.
2. Be selective about your words.
3. Listen for opportunities to speak positively about something that may be a challenge for your friends, co-workers or family.

JOURNAL:

What is the most encouraging thing anyone has ever done for you? Pray and ask God how you can be a blessing to someone by encouraging them. Write a few scriptures that can be used to encourage someone.

_____
_____
_____
_____
_____
_____
_____
_____
_____
_____
_____
_____
_____
_____

ENDURE

DEFINITION: To bear without resistance or with patience; tolerance.

DISCUSSION QUESTIONS:

1. Discuss a challenging situation you endured.

2. What are the benefits of enduring?

3. What are the challenges of enduring hardship and rejection?

LOOK IN THE WORD:

1. Read I Corinthians 13:7. "Love endures all things." What do ALL things mean to you?

2. How can having a relationship with Jesus help one to endure?

APPLICATION:

1. Ask God for the grace to endure.
2. Commit all of your challenges, hardships or any time you were mistreated to God.
3. Maintain daily time with the Lord through prayer and reading scripture.

JOURNAL:

Jesus Christ suffered, bled and died for us. He endured the pain of the cross; therefore, He knows what it is to endure. Write your thoughts about enduring. Explain what enduring means to you.

ENTERTAINING

DEFINITION: To have as a guest; provide food or lodging; to exercise hospitality.

DISCUSSION QUESTIONS:

1. When was the last time you invited guests into your home?

2. What special arrangements/preparations did you make for your guests?

3. Discuss some of the ways you demonstrate hospitality.

4. How do you think people feel when they have entered your home?

LOOK IN THE WORD:

1. Read Romans 12:13 and Hebrews 13:2. What does it mean to be given to "hospitality?" Are you given to hospitality? Why or why not?

2. Based on Hebrews 13:2, what are some benefits to practicing hospitality?

APPLICATION:

1. Be intentional about inviting guests into your home.
2. Clean your home (or have someone else to) on a regular basis.
3. Be sure that your home is ready to receive guests at any time.
4. Assign chores so that everyone who lives in your house has responsibilities.

JOURNAL:

Why do you think the Lord wants us to be given to hospitality? How can entertaining provide an avenue for us to show the love of God?

CHAPTER SIX
THE F PRINCIPLES

FAITHFUL

DEFINITION: True to one's words, vows or promises.

DISCUSSION QUESTIONS:

1. God is so faithful. List some of the ways God has been faithful in your life.

   _____
   _____
   _____

2. Read the *Faithful Principle*. Explain what it means to be faithful to your family, friends or your calling.

   _____
   _____
   _____

3. What are some of the consequences of being unfaithful?

   _____
   _____
   _____

LOOK IN THE WORD:

1. Read Luke 16:10. How can this verse apply to your life?

   _____
   _____
   _____

2. What areas in your life can you begin to practice faithfulness before getting married?

   _____
   _____
   _____

APPLICATION:

1. Be sure that you are faithful in spending intimate time with the Lord.
2. Ask God for the grace to be faithful during your season of singleness. Imitate Christ. Just as He is faithful to you, be faithful to Him.
3. Find joy and satisfaction in Jesus. Ask God to help you to control your physical desires and to meet your every need. Whenever you struggle, pray and find an accountability partner.

JOURNAL:

How is God speaking to you about the *Faithful Principle*? Can you be faithful to Jesus, your friends or your calling? Why or why not?

_____
_____
_____
_____
_____
_____
_____
_____
_____
_____
_____
_____
_____
_____
_____
_____

FINANCES

DEFINITION: The conduct or transaction of money matters.

DISCUSSION QUESTIONS:

1. What can you do financially to help prepare yourself for marriage?

   _____
   _____
   _____

2. Are you in debt? If so, what can you do to start getting out of debt?

   _____
   _____
   _____

3. Review the *Finance Principle* and list three out of the five lessons the author mentions under this principle. Which lesson stands out most to you and why?

   _____
   _____
   _____

3. What do you think about operating from a joint account? Are you willing?

   _____
   _____
   _____

LOOK IN THE WORD:

1. Find a scripture which applies to any of the five lessons mentioned in the *Finance Principle*.

   _____
   _____
   _____

2. Read the scripture, discuss or write what God is speaking to you.

   _____
   _____
   _____

APPLICATION:

1. If you have not done so, create a budget. Make a list of everything coming in and going out.
2. Set financial goals.
3. If you desire to have a wedding, establish a savings account specifically for the expenses.

JOURNAL:

What is a lesson you have learned concerning your finances? What changes have you made as a result of the lessons learned?

_____
_____
_____
_____
_____
_____
_____
_____
_____
_____
_____
_____
_____
_____
_____
_____

FORGIVENESS

DEFINITION: To cease to feel resentment against. To forgive.

DISCUSSION QUESTIONS:

1. Read the *Forgiveness Principle*. (pages 33-34) How would you have handled having a stolen IPOD?

2. "Forgiveness is a choice." What does this mean to you?

3. God forgives us daily. How does it feel to be forgiven? When someone has hurt you, do you typically let them know or do you keep silent and hold it against them?

4. Is there anyone in your life who you need to forgive or ask forgiveness from?

LOOK IN THE WORD:

1. Read Matthew 6:14. What does God want us to do?

2. Based on this scripture, why is it so important to forgive?

APPLICATION:

1. Think of a situation where forgiveness is needed. Choose to forgive.
2. Call, write or connect with the person who you need to forgive or ask forgiveness from. Ask them to forgive or grant forgiveness.
3. Be quick to forgive; don't carry issues for a long time.

JOURNAL:

What is your normal response to hurt? Do you forgive or hold a grudge? Why? Are you willing to obey God and forgive?

FRIENDSHIP

DEFINITION: The state of being friends (a person attached to another by feelings or affection).

DISCUSSION QUESTIONS:

1. Think about your closest friends. Would you being married change any of these relationships? How?

   _____
   _____
   _____

2. Do you have any close friends who are married? Have you been able to learn anything from observing their marriage?

   _____
   _____
   _____

3. What are the keys to having a good friendship?

   _____
   _____
   _____

LOOK IN THE WORD:

1. Read Proverbs 17:17. What does this scripture mean to you?

   _____
   _____
   _____

2. How can you apply this scripture to your friendships?

   _____
   _____
   _____

APPLICATION:

1. Remember, if you want to have friends, you must first show yourself as friendly.
2. Be intentional about setting aside time for you to get together with friends.
3. Create a safe place with each other so that your friends will feel comfortable sharing with you.

JOURNAL:

What is your idea of having a good friendship?

CHAPTER SEVEN
THE G PRINCIPLES

GIVE

DEFINITION: To put into the possession of another.

DISCUSSION QUESTIONS:

1. How can you give to others?

2. What passion has God placed in your heart? How can the passion be used to help others?

3. How do you feel when you are a blessing to others?

4. Share an experience where someone gave you their time, money or their presence. How did it feel?

LOOK IN THE WORD:

1. Read Luke 6:38. What are the instructions in this scripture?

2. What are some of the blessings in giving?

APPLICATION:

1. Be intentional about giving of yourself, your time and money to bless others.
2. Discuss something you could do regularly to give to others.
3. Give cheerfully in a way that brings glory and honor to God.
4. Think about another single friend you might be a blessing to; invite them over for dinner.

JOURNAL:

What is God saying to you about giving? What are some of the things God has given to you? What can you give to others?

___
___
___
___
___
___
___
___
___
___
___
___
___
___
___

GOALS

DEFINITION: The end towards which effort is directed.

DISCUSSION QUESTIONS:

1. Write one personal goal you would like to accomplish this year.

   _____
   _____
   _____

2. What are some disciplines which need to be practiced in order to accomplish the goal?

   _____
   _____
   _____

3. How can you support a friend to help him/her reach their goal?

   _____
   _____
   _____

LOOK IN THE WORD:

1. Read Philippians 3:14. What does the Word say about reaching a goal?

   _____
   _____
   _____

2. What does it mean to press?

   _____
   _____
   _____

APPLICATION:

1. Create a Goal Journal. Write down goals that you would like to accomplish.
2. Establish a date for accomplishing your goals.
3. Be intentional about supporting your friends and family.
4. Discipline yourself so the goal can be accomplished.

JOURNAL:

What are your thoughts about setting goals? How are you doing with setting and achieving your goals?

GOD

DEFINITION: The one Supreme Being, the creator and ruler of the universe.

DISCUSSION QUESTIONS:

1. Do you include God in your daily life? Tell how.

2. How could you include Him more?

3. We are here to glorify God with our mind, body and soul. Explain how your life is fulfilling this purpose.

LOOK IN THE WORD:

1. Read Ecclesiastes 4:12. What do you think about a threefold cord?

2. How does this cord relate to a marriage relationship?

APPLICATION:

1. Pray daily.
2. Be intentional about including God in your life through prayer, scripture reading and worship.
3. Apply the Word of God to your life.
4. Obey the Word. Just do it!

JOURNAL:

God wants to be included in every part of your life. How do you include Him?

GODLY SEEDS

DEFINITION: Children who are raised in the fear of the Lord.

DISCUSSION QUESTIONS:

1. According to the *Godly Seeds Principle*, what is the most powerful way to raise a godly seed?

2. Do you have children? If so, have you taught your children about Jesus? Are you living a Christian life before them? If you don't have children, pray about being a blessing to someone else's children.

3. What is the difference between a child who has been taught the Word of God and a child who has not been taught?

LOOK IN THE WORD:

1. Read Deuteronomy 6:6-7. What is the message to parents?

2. How can you share Christ with your children?

APPLICATION:

1. Pray daily for children in your family and children in general.
2. Share scripture with children.
3. Invite a child and their parents to church, Sunday school or a children's youth group.
4. Live a Christian life before them.

JOURNAL:

What is a godly seed? Why is it important for children to be taught about God?

_____
_____
_____
_____
_____
_____
_____
_____
_____
_____
_____
_____
_____
_____
_____
_____
_____

CHAPTER EIGHT
THE H PRINCIPLES

HEALTH

DEFINITION: The condition of being sound, in body, mind or spirit.

DISCUSSION QUESTIONS:

1. What are you doing to practice good health?

   _____
   _____
   _____

2. Do you have friends or family who will hold you accountable to living healthy?

   _____
   _____
   _____

3. Evaluate how you are doing in the following areas: eating, resting, exercising, regular doctor visits, etc.

   _____
   _____
   _____

LOOK IN THE WORD:

1. Read III John 2. What is John's prayer request?

   _____
   _____
   _____

2. Why is it important to be in good health?

   _____
   _____
   _____

APPLICATION:

1. Think of one change you know you need to make in order to have better health.
2. Commit to exercising at home, in the gym or walking in a neighborhood with a friend.
3. Make healthier food choices.
4. Make a doctor's appointment annually.

JOURNAL:

Examine your health. What is God saying to you about maintaining good health?

HELPER

DEFINITION: A person or thing that helps.

DISCUSSION QUESTIONS:

1. What are the characteristics of a good helper?
   _____
   _____
   _____

2. List ways in which you enjoy helping others.
   _____
   _____
   _____

3. How can you help a friend or family member reach a desired destination or goal?
   _____
   _____
   _____

LOOK IN THE WORD:

1. Read Genesis 2:18. What does it mean to have a helper "comparable to him?"
   _____
   _____
   _____

2. Do you consider yourself to be a good helper?
   _____
   _____
   _____

APPLICATION:

1. Ask your friends or family how you could help more.
2. Be sure to have quiet time with the Lord. Ask God to teach you how to be the best helper that you can be.
3. Examine your conduct. Have you been a good helper? How can you be a better helper?

JOURNAL:

What is your conduct like? Are you helping or hurting others?

HONEY

DEFINITION: Something sweet, delicious or delightful.

DISCUSSION QUESTIONS:

1. What does the statement "keep the honey in the moon" mean to you?

2. If adding honey can make a situation sweeter, what makes it sour? Give an example.

3. What act of kindness can you do to please God and to bless your friends and family?

LOOK IN THE WORD:

1. Read Jeremiah 31:3. Jesus drew people with loving kindness. How should we draw others closer?

2. Read Song of Solomon 4:15-5:1. Solomon says "I have eaten my honey comb and my honey." Discuss. Who or what is Solomon referring to?

APPLICATION:

1. Reflect on some of your current friendships, and think about things that can be done to put more honey into them.
2. Strive to be sweet to others.
   » give an encouraging word
   » smile
   » give an unexpected gift
   » write a nice card or call instead of texting/emailing a friend

JOURNAL:

Have you tasted honey? Use 2-3 words to describe honey. Write about what you could do to put more honey in your relationships.

_____
_____
_____
_____
_____
_____
_____
_____
_____
_____
_____
_____
_____
_____
_____
_____

HOUSEWORK

DEFINITION: The work of cooking, cleaning, etc.

DISCUSSION QUESTIONS:

1. Is your house ready to receive guests today?

   _____
   _____
   _____

2. If unexpected guests were coming to your house, would you be able to welcome them or would you have to clean your house first?

   _____
   _____
   _____

3. Is keeping a clean and orderly home necessary? Why or why not?

   _____
   _____
   _____

LOOK IN THE WORD:

1. Read Titus 2:4. What is your idea of a homemaker?

   _____
   _____
   _____

2. How can this verse be applied in your household?

   _____
   _____
   _____

APPLICATION:

1. Maintain a home prepared to receive guests, by cleaning as you go.
2. Be sure everyone who lives in your house has assigned chores to help maintain a clean house.
3. Practice putting things back in their proper places, and teach your children (if you have them) to do the same.

JOURNAL:

What are the rooms in your house saying? How are you doing with maintaining a clean home?

CHAPTER NINE
THE I PRINCIPLES

IN TUNE

DEFINITION: In concord (harmony) or agreement between persons.

DISCUSSION QUESTIONS:

1. Are you in tune with God?

2. Are there any issues on your heart that bother you, and for whatever reason, you have not discussed them with God?

3. What can you do to become more in tune with God?

LOOK IN THE WORD:

1. Read Proverbs 3:6. According to the first part of this verse, what should be your goal with God?

2. How does acknowledging God make us more in tune with Him?

APPLICATION:

1. Spend regular time with God.
2. Study God's Word. Learn how to apply God's Word to every situation in your life.
3. Listen to God's voice and obey.
4. Pray throughout the day.

JOURNAL:

What does it mean to be in tune with God? How can spending time alone with the Lord make you more in tune with Him?

INITIATE

DEFINITION: To begin, to set or originate.

DISCUSSION QUESTIONS:

1. When was the last time you initiated extra time with God?

2. What normally initiates your time with God; a class, a fast, a crisis or you?

3. When you see someone who you would like to get to know, will you initiate speaking?

4. When it comes to doing a job, are you usually a person who takes initiative or do you have to be asked?

LOOK IN THE WORD:

1. Read Matthew 26:41. This verse states that, "we're to watch and pray. . . that the spirit is willing but the flesh is weak." What does this verse mean to you?

2. How will initiating time with God help us to fulfill this scripture?

APPLICATION:

1. Initiate more. God loves when we come to Him.
2. Prepare your mind to initiate (pray, read, listen to music).
3. Include God in your everyday routine. Pray and ask Him to bless the time with him.

JOURNAL:

How is God speaking to you about the *Initiate Principle*? When you are in a social setting, are you normally the person who initiates speaking? Why or why not?

_____
_____
_____
_____
_____
_____
_____
_____
_____
_____
_____
_____
_____
_____
_____
_____
_____

INTIMACY

DEFINITION: Close, familiar and usually affectionate or loving personal relationship with another person.

DISCUSSION QUESTIONS:

1. What does intimacy mean to you?

2. Do you feel that you are intimate with God? Why or why not?

3. What helps you to feel intimate with God?

4. What makes you feel distant from God?

LOOK IN THE WORD:

1. Read James 4:8. How does this verse relate to your intimacy with God?

2. What are the benefits of intimacy?

3. How does intimacy help to strengthen your relationship with God?

APPLICATION:

1. Develop intimacy with God through prayer, reading the word and spending time with Him. As you spend time with God, He will reveal things about you and the relationships that are closest to you.

2. Spend regular time in God's presence. Talk and share your innermost thoughts.

3. If there is a wall blocking the intimacy between you and God, find out what it is and pray for ways to tear the wall down. Trust God to restore your intimacy with Him this year!

JOURNAL:

Our God is a jealous God. He wants us to be intimate with Him first. How are you doing with spending intimate time with the Lord? What is God saying to you about intimacy?

_____
_____
_____
_____
_____
_____
_____
_____
_____
_____
_____
_____
_____
_____

ISOLATION

DEFINITION: To set or place apart. To separate or be alone.

DISCUSSION QUESTIONS:

1. Do you ever isolate yourself from relationships? Why or why not?

   _____
   _____
   _____

2. For married people, isolation + separation = divorce. For singles, isolation + separation = disaster or discouragement. What are your thoughts about isolation and separation?

   _____
   _____
   _____

3. What causes isolation? Is there anything isolating you from your friends and family?

   _____
   _____
   _____

4. What can you do to prevent isolation?

   _____
   _____
   _____

LOOK IN THE WORD:

1. The Bible says that two are better than one. (Ecclesiastes 4:9) What does this verse mean to you?

   _____
   _____
   _____

2. How does isolation contradict this verse?

   _____
   _____
   _____

APPLICATION:

1. Pray when you feel yourself moving toward isolation.
2. Discuss your feelings with a close friend. Strive to move closer to God rather than further apart.
3. Try to get to the root of the desire to isolate.

JOURNAL:

Are you isolating yourself from others? If so, write about your feelings and submit them to God. If not, write a prayer of thanksgiving to God.

CHAPTER TEN
THE J PRINCIPLES

JESUS

DEFINITION: The Son of God, our Savior and Lord.

DISCUSSION QUESTIONS:

1. Do you have a personal relationship with Jesus?

2. Have you invited Jesus into every aspect of your life?

3. How can you get to know Jesus better?

4. How does having a relationship with Jesus make a difference in you and others?

LOOK IN THE WORD:

1. Read Romans 10:13. What does it say about being saved?

2. How do you know that you are saved? Find a scripture to support your answer.

APPLICATION:

1. If you are not saved, invite Jesus into your heart. (Romans 3:10, 3:23, 6:23 and 10:9-10).

2. Include Jesus in your everyday life through prayer and reading the Bible and commit to going to a local church.

3. Learn the ways of Jesus and imitate Him in all you do.

JOURNAL:

Jesus came to bring us life more abundantly (John 10:10). How has Jesus made a difference in your life?

_____
_____
_____
_____
_____
_____
_____
_____
_____
_____
_____
_____
_____
_____

JOINT ACCOUNTS

DEFINITION: A bank account in the names of two or more persons or parties subject to withdrawal by each.

DISCUSSION QUESTIONS:

1. Do you operate your finances from a joint perspective, allowing God to be an intricate part of them? Why or why not?

2. What are some challenges that may come with joining your money with another individual? (potential spouse)

3. Based on the *"Joint Account" Principle*, why is it important for a husband and wife to join their money?

4. How does communication help in operating a joint account?

LOOK IN THE WORD:

1. Read Genesis 2:24. Explain how this verse relates to joint accounts.

2. Why do you think oneness is important to God?

APPLICATION:

1. If you do not have a joint account with God, establish one.
2. Wait until you are married to join your money with a potential spouse.
3. Pray regularly about your saving and spending habits.

JOURNAL:

How are you doing with carrying out this principle? What are your thoughts about the *Joint Account Principle*? (page 51)

JOY

DEFINITION: The emotion of great delight or happiness caused by something exceptionally good or satisfying.

DISCUSSION QUESTIONS:

1. Do you have joy, even when life doesn't go as planned?

2. What is the difference between happiness and joy?

3. Have you experienced the joy of the Lord?

4. How could you have or experience more joy?

LOOK IN THE WORD:

1. Read John 15:11. What are the two things that are mentioned in this verse?

2. Nehemiah 8:10 says, the joy of the Lord shall be our strength. Explain how we can have joy all the time.

APPLICATION:

1. Spend daily time with the Lord. He wants to give you permanent joy.
2. Reflect on the blessings of God every day. Start your day focusing on the many blessings of God (life, health, strength, food, clothing, shelter, eyes to see, ears to hear, feet to walk, etc.)
3. Read Philippians 4:8 on a regular basis. Reflect on what this verse means.

JOURNAL:

Do you have joy? After reading the scriptures on joy, what can you do to get more joy?"

CHAPTER ELEVEN
THE K PRINCIPLES

KEEPING IT TOGETHER

DEFINITION: Maintain yourself from the inside out.

DISCUSSION QUESTIONS:

1. How are you doing with maintaining your outward appearance (hair, body, clothing, etc.)?

2. Do you think God is pleased with your appearance? (If you don't know, ask.)

3. What steps are you willing to take to make changes where change is needed?

LOOK IN THE WORD:

1. Read I Peter 3:3. Explain the message that is given in I Peter 3:3. Based on this verse, what should be our primary focus?

2. Ladies, what can you do to work on your inner beauty? Men, what can you do to maintain your inner self?

APPLICATION:

1. Evaluate yourself from the inside out. Ask yourself, " is God pleased with the inner me?"
2. Remember to keep yourself together by taking time for you, keeping your hair groomed, being mindful of the food that you eat and the clothes that you wear.
3. Improve the inner you by spending time reading God's Word and being obedient to His Word.
4. Improve the outer you by exercising, eating healthy foods and being a little more selective about what you wear.

JOURNAL:

How do you keep it together? Is this an area of struggle or are you pleased with how you are doing?

KINDNESS

DEFINITION: The state or quality of being kind (considerate, helpful, gentle).

DISCUSSION QUESTIONS:

1. How do you normally respond when you have to suffer or endure difficult situations?

   _____
   _____
   _____

2. What does kindness look like to you?

   _____
   _____
   _____

3. How can you display more kindness toward those who hurt or disappoint you?

   _____
   _____
   _____

4. Evaluate your actions this week. Have you displayed kindness to difficult people? How?

   _____
   _____
   _____

LOOK IN THE WORD:

1. Read I Corinthians 13:4. Love suffers long and is kind. Give an example of how one can suffer and still be kind.

   _____
   _____
   _____

2. Read Galatians 5:22. Fill in the blank:

   But the fruit of the Spirit is love, joy, peace, longsuffering, _____, goodness, faithfulness, gentleness and self-control. Against such is no law.

APPLICATION:

1. Express kindness in a different way today.
2. Share something that you have with a friend, neighbor or co-worker.
3. Do something kind that you don't normally do.
4. Cook a meal or dessert for a friend, neighbor or co-worker.
5. Intentionally be kind to others each day.
6. Remember that Jesus uses kindness to draw people to Him. Imitate Jesus!

JOURNAL:

What is one of the kindest things that anyone has ever done for you?

_____
_____
_____
_____
_____
_____
_____
_____
_____
_____
_____
_____
_____
_____

KING

DEFINITION: A male sovereign; the husband.

DISCUSSION QUESTIONS:

1. Is Jesus Christ the King of your life? What can you do to treat Him like a King?

2. (Ladies) What is your idea of treating a man like a king?

3. (Gentlemen) What is your idea of being treated like a king?

LOOK IN THE WORD:

1. Read the following verses: Psalm 10:16, Psalm 24:7, Psalm 74:12, Jeremiah 10:10, Revelation 19:16. What do these verses tell us about our King of Kings?

2. Read I Peter 3:1. According to this verse, how can God use a wife's conduct?

APPLICATION:

1. Discover what pleases your King of Kings and do it.
2. Show honor and reverence to the King of Kings by praying, reading the Bible, worshiping and applying God's Word to your life.

JOURNAL:

How is your relationship with the King of Kings and the Lord of Lords?

KISSING

DEFINITION: To join lips in respect, affection, love, passion, etc.

DISCUSSION QUESTIONS:

1. Should kissing be done while dating or should it be saved for marriage?
   _____
   _____
   _____

2. As a single, how might kissing be a stumbling block?
   _____
   _____
   _____

3. How would you discuss kissing with someone who has an opposing view?
   _____
   _____
   _____

LOOK IN THE WORD:

1. Read Song of Solomon 1:2. Fill in the blanks.
   _____
   _____
   _____

2. Let him _____ me with the _____ of his mouth.

3. The Shulamite woman was welcoming a kiss from her husband. What can you learn from this?
   _____
   _____
   _____

APPLICATION:

1. Save kissing for marriage.
2. Don't do anything that will light your fire (stimulate sexual desires).
3. Memorize Song of Solomon 8:4.

JOURNAL:

Do you think passionate kissing is just for the movies? Why or why not?

CHAPTER TWELVE
THE L PRINCIPLES

LEAVE AND CLEAVE

DEFINITION: To detach from your parents and cling to your spouse.

DISCUSSION QUESTIONS:

1. Review the *Leave and Cleave Principle* (page 57) and explain what it means to you.

2. What are some problems that may occur when a spouse does not leave and cleave?

3. What may hinder you from being able to leave and cleave successfully?

4. What does it mean to leave the world and cleave to God?

LOOK IN THE WORD:

1. Read Genesis 2:24. What are the instructions given in this verse?

2. Who is this verse speaking to?

3. Why do you think God wants a man to leave and cleave?

   _____
   _____
   _____

APPLICATION:

1. Examine yourself. Is there anything that you need to leave in order to cleave more to God? Also, to your potential spouse?

2. Ask your parents or someone close to you if there is something that you need to leave in order to prepare to cleave to your potential spouse.

JOURNAL:

How is God speaking to you about the *Leave and Cleave Principle*? (page 57) Is this an issue for you or someone that you know? If so, pray for them.

_____
_____
_____
_____
_____
_____
_____
_____
_____
_____
_____
_____
_____
_____

LOVE

DEFINITION: A feeling of warm personal attachment or deep affection for another person.

DISCUSSION QUESTIONS:

1. Is it difficult for you to say, "I love you"?

   _____
   _____
   _____

2. What makes you feel loved?

   _____
   _____
   _____

3. How can you use your actions to let your friends, family or a potential spouse know that you love them?

   _____
   _____
   _____

LOOK IN THE WORD:

1. Review I Corinthians 13. Write down some attributes of love.

   _____
   _____
   _____

2. Create a T chart and label one side "Love Do's" and the other side "Love Does Not."
   Fill in the chart based on what I Corinthians 13 says about love.

   _____
   _____
   _____

APPLICATION:

1. Practice demonstrating love to your family, friends and your enemies.
2. Read Gary Chapman's book *"The Five Love Languages."* Discover your love language.
3. Write a love letter to someone you love.

JOURNAL:

In this principle, the author mentions loving regardless of the circumstances. We can only get this type of love from the Lord. What does loving regardless of the circumstances mean to you?

CHAPTER THIRTEEN
THE M PRINCIPLES

MANAGE

DEFINITION: To take charge or care of.

DISCUSSION QUESTIONS:

1. Evaluate yourself: Are you pleased with the way that you are managing your life and your home?

2. What do you manage best? What are some of your challenges?

3. If you have children, how can they help with managing and maintaining the home?

LOOK IN THE WORD:

1. Proverbs 31:27 says that the virtuous wife watches over the ways of her household. As a single, how are you watching over your household?

2. What seems to be working well in your household? What needs to be better managed?

APPLICATION:

1. Develop your managing skills while you are single.
2. Maintain a family calendar. Keep a visible list of all of the events and appointments for everyone.
3. Work on developing areas that you feel you are weak in.
4. Evaluate how you manage the finances, schedule and keeping the house in order. Are there any changes that need to be made?

JOURNAL:

How are you doing with managing your life and your home? Do you think God is pleased? Why or why not?

_____
_____
_____
_____
_____
_____
_____
_____
_____
_____
_____
_____
_____
_____
_____
_____

MANNERS

DEFINITION: The way that we behave with reference to polite standards.

DISCUSSION QUESTIONS:

1. Do you treat your guests special when they enter your home for the first time? What are some of the things you may do for a guest?

   _____
   _____
   _____

2. Do you use manners when you are out with friends and family (being considerate, saying please, thank you and no thank you, etc.)?

   _____
   _____
   _____

3. Are manners important to you? Why or why not?

   _____
   _____
   _____

LOOK IN THE WORD:

1. Read I Corinthians 13:4-5. Examine how you treat others. Do you behave in a kind way or do you behave rudely?

   _____
   _____
   _____

2. What is God's expectation for how we should conduct ourselves?

   _____
   _____
   _____

APPLICATION:

1. Be intentional about using your manners with the people in your life.
2. Offer to do something for your friends, family, and co-workers that you would not normally do.
3. Practice saying thank you or I appreciate you doing _____.
4. Be considerate.
5. If you are a man, practice opening the doors for ladies and giving up your seat when applicable.

JOURNAL:

How are you doing with displaying manners towards others? How can you do better?

MIRROR

DEFINITION: Any reflecting surface used in viewing oneself.

DISCUSSION QUESTIONS:

1. When you look in a mirror, what do you see?

   _____
   _____
   _____

2. Does your relationship with others reflect the love of God?

   _____
   _____
   _____

3. What can you do to make yourself mirror Christ?

   _____
   _____
   _____

LOOK IN THE WORD:

1. Read Genesis 1:27. Fill in the blanks: So God created _____, in His own _____; in the _____ of God He created him; _____ and _____ He created them.

2. Who should your relationships with others and your future marriage reflect?

   _____
   _____
   _____

APPLICATION:

1. Practice displaying the love of Christ in your everyday relationships.
2. Share the love of Christ with others.
3. Spend time reading God's Word and praying. The more you spend time with the Lord, the more you learn about His ways of thinking and serving.

JOURNAL:

Write a detailed description of what you see when you look in the mirror and what you would like for others to see.

_____
_____
_____
_____
_____
_____
_____
_____
_____
_____
_____
_____
_____
_____
_____
_____

MULTIPLY

DEFINITION: To make many or increase in number.

DISCUSSION QUESTIONS:

1. Read the *Multiply Principle*. (pages 63-64) What are the two things that the author was told about multiplying?

2. Can you identify with either? Why or why not?

3. Is there anything in your life that you would like to multiply? Why or why not?

LOOK IN THE WORD:

1. Read Genesis 1:22 and Psalm 127:5. What does this scripture say about multiplying?

2. Compare God's view towards multiplying and the world's view. What is the difference?

APPLICATION:

1. Think about whether or not you want to be fruitful and multiply when you are married.
2. If you are not able to get pregnant once you are married, would you be willing to consider helping someone to care for their children, or adopting a child?
3. Eat healthy and exercise to prepare your body for multiplying.

JOURNAL:

What does it mean to be fruitful and multiply? Why do you think the scripture says be fruitful, and then multiply?

CHAPTER FOURTEEN
THE N PRINCIPLES

NAGGING

DEFINITION: Continually faultfinding, complaining or petulant.

DISCUSSION QUESTIONS:

1. What is nagging? Give an example.

2. Based on the *Nagging Principle* (page 65), does nagging have a positive or negative effect?

3. Have you ever experienced being nagged or witnessed someone else nagging their spouse? How did it make you feel?

4. What can you do to make sure that you do not nag?

LOOK IN THE WORD:

1. Read Proverbs 21:9 and Proverbs 21:19. What message can you get from these two verses?

2. How can these verses be applied in your relationships with others?

APPLICATION:

1. Examine yourself. Are you a nagger? If so, ask God to teach you how to tame your tongue.
2. If nagging has been a habit, practice saying less and praying more.
3. If you have been a nagger to anyone in your life, apologize to them and let them know you are striving to be better with the Lord's help.
4. Ask God to make you sensitive to the nagging spirit so that you can stop yourself before you speak.

JOURNAL:

Before reading this principle, did you know that the Bible addresses a nagging wife? Why is it important for every woman to understand the impact of nagging?

_____
_____
_____
_____
_____
_____
_____
_____
_____
_____
_____
_____
_____
_____
_____
_____

NEGATIVE

DEFINITION: Expressing or containing negation or denial.

DISCUSSION QUESTIONS:
1. What does it mean to be negative?

2. Examine your friendships. Are there any friends who constantly speak negatively?

3. How can negative talk, feelings and emotions impact your relationships with others?

4. What can you do to avoid speaking negatively?

LOOK IN THE WORD:
1. Read Ephesians 4:29. What does this verse say about our communication?

2. How can you apply this verse to your life?

APPLICATION:
1. Be mindful of the words that come out of your mouth. Speak positively!
2. Pray about any negative thoughts that come to your mind.
3. Focus on the positive in friends, family and co-workers.

JOURNAL:

Imagine if Christ only focused on our negatives. Make a list of all of the positive traits that you have. Explain how these traits can be used to bless someone else.

NOTICE

DEFINITION: To pay attention to, be aware of or to acknowledge.

DISCUSSION QUESTIONS:

1. Have you ever experienced getting a new haircut, color, or style and no one seemed to have noticed? How did you feel?

2. Are you normally good about noticing and then giving a compliment to people in your life?

3. What is something that you wish people would notice about you?

LOOK IN THE WORD:

1. Read Song of Solomon 7:1-9. What does the husband notice about his wife's body? What does he say?

2. How can taking time to notice something about the people in your life make a difference in your everyday relationships?

APPLICATION:

1. Be observant and notice friends, family and co-workers.
2. Give compliments when compliments are due. Don't hold back.

JOURNAL:

Throughout the Bible, Jesus is known for taking the time to notice people and recognizing details about them. What do you think about the *Notice Principle*?

_____
_____
_____
_____
_____
_____
_____
_____
_____
_____
_____
_____
_____
_____
_____
_____

NOURISH

DEFINITION: To sustain with food or nutriment.

DISCUSSION QUESTIONS:

1. Based on this principle (page 67), what does it mean to nourish?

   _____
   _____
   _____

2. Do you feel you were properly nourished as a child? Why or why not?

   _____
   _____
   _____

3. Do you feel that you would do a good job of nourishing someone else? Why or why not?

   _____
   _____
   _____

LOOK IN THE WORD:

1. Read Ephesians 5:28-29. Fill in the blanks. So _____ ought to _____ their own _____ as their own _____, he who _____ his _____ loves himself. For no one ever _____ his own _____, but _____ and _____ it, just as the _____ does the church.

APPLICATION:

1. Ask God to teach you how to be nourishing to others.
2. If you have children, ask God to teach you how to nourish your children so that they can learn how to nourish others.
3. If you desire to be married, ask God to send you a spouse who is nourishing.

JOURNAL:

If a person is malnourished as a child, how will he know how to nourish as an adult? How might this impact their marriage relationship?

CHAPTER FIFTEEN
THE O PRINCIPLES

OBEDIENCE

DEFINITION: Being willing to obey, to follow the instructions, the commands or the wishes of someone else.

DISCUSSION QUESTIONS:

1. Write two rules that you remember being told when you were a child (either in school or at home).

2. Are you good at following rules or instructions? Why or why not?

3. List two instructions that God has given through His Word.

4. How are you doing with following God's instructions?

LOOK IN THE WORD:

1. Read Deuteronomy 28:1-2. Based on this scripture, what are the benefits of obedience?

2. Read Joshua 1:8. How can you make your way prosperous and have good success?

APPLICATION:

1. Spend time learning God's instructions (read the Word, take a class, study to show yourself approved).
2. Practice applying the Word to your everyday life.
3. Listen to the Holy Spirit.
4. Don't do things that are contrary to the Word of God.

JOURNAL:

Think about your relationship with the Lord. Is there anything that He has placed on your heart to do and you have not done? Ask the Lord to forgive you and be obedient. Write a prayer to the Lord.

ON TIME

DEFINITION: At the scheduled or proper time, to be punctual.

DISCUSSION QUESTIONS:

1. The *On Time Principle* (page 70) is very simple. What is the main point of this principle?

2. Are you normally on time or late for events? How would you like to be remembered? ("Always Late" or "Always on Time")

3. Do you know of friends who are always late? What suggestions could you give for helping them to arrive on time?

4. What are some of the disadvantages to being late for events and the advantages for being on time?

LOOK IN THE WORD:

1. Read Ecclesiastes 3:1. What does this verse tell us about time?

2. Why should we strive to be on time when attending an event, meeting, going to work or anywhere?

APPLICATION:

1. Don't schedule too much on one day.
2. Find out how much time it takes to get to an event and plan accordingly.
3. Allow yourself more than enough time.
4. Strive to be ahead of time.
5. Get directions ahead of time or be sure that your navigational system is correct.

JOURNAL:

Jesus may not come when you want Him, but He is always right on time. Write about a time where Jesus came or helped you right on time.

___

___

___

___

___

___

___

___

___

___

___

___

___

___

OPEN

DEFINITION: Unreserved or candid. Ready to entertain new ideas; not biased or prejudiced.

DISCUSSION QUESTIONS:

1. Is there anyone in your life who you feel safe to be open with?

2. Are you holding things in that really should be discussed? Explain your answer.

3. How do you think being open can benefit your relationship with a potential spouse?

4. Are you open for what God has in store for your life?

LOOK IN THE WORD:

1. Read Genesis 2:25. Do you feel you can be naked and not ashamed with a good friend or your potential spouse?

2. Is there anything from your past that makes you hesitant to share openly?

APPLICATION:

1. Talk to an appropriate person about strongholds you have that could hold you back from being open.
2. Be open to the plans God has for you. Pray about every opportunity presented.
3. Pray to God for a spouse who is willing to be open.

JOURNAL:

What does it mean to be naked and not ashamed?

OPEN DOORS

DEFINITION: Admission to; access.

DISCUSSION QUESTIONS:

1. Men – Are you accustomed to opening doors for women?
   _____
   _____
   _____

2. Women – Are you accustomed to men opening doors for you?
   _____
   _____
   _____

3. How do you think serving in this manner can bring glory and honor to God?
   _____
   _____
   _____

LOOK IN THE WORD:

1. Read Mark 10:35-45. What does Jesus say about serving? How can this apply to your life?
   _____
   _____
   _____

2. Fill in the blank (verse 45). "For even the _____ of _____ did not come to be _____, but to _____, and to give His life a ransom for many."

APPLICATION:

1. Men – If you are not opening the doors for women, try it.
2. Women – Allow men to open doors for you. Be patient and wait.
3. Look for ways to serve others.
4. Serve others with the right attitude. Serve with a smile.

JOURNAL:

Opening doors is just one way to serve. What are other ways you can serve and that you would like to be served?

CHAPTER SIXTEEN
THE P PRINCIPLES

PARENTS

DEFINITION: A father, mother or guardian.

DISCUSSION QUESTIONS:

1. What type of relationship do you have with your parents? (close, distant or non-existent)

2. What is one lesson that you have learned from your parents in reference to relationships?

3. If you have a potential spouse, have your parents met him/her? What are their thoughts?

4. Examine your relationship with your parents. Are you relying on your parents to do things that you should be doing yourself?

LOOK IN THE WORD:

1. Read Ephesians 4:29. Fill in the blanks. Let no _____ word proceed _____ of your _____, but what is _____ for necessary _____, that it may impart _____ to the _____.

2. How can applying this verse make a difference in what you choose to tell your parents or anyone else about your potential spouse?

APPLICATION:

1. Realize that your parents are an authority in your life, and God does speak through them.
2. If possible, get your parents' blessings when you are considering marriage.
3. Remember that you will not be able to rely on your parents to do some things when you get married. Some responsibilities will shift to your spouse.

JOURNAL:

Honor your father and your mother, that your days may be long upon the land which the Lord your God is given you. (Exodus 20:12) How can you honor your parents? How can you ensure that there is a good relationship between your parents and your potential spouse?

_____
_____
_____
_____
_____
_____
_____
_____
_____
_____
_____
_____
_____
_____
_____
_____

PHONE CALLS

DEFINITION: To speak to by summon or telephone; to send a message.

DISCUSSION QUESTIONS:

1. Based on this principle (See page 74), how can the telephone be used to help the communication in your relationships?

2. How often do you use the phone to call someone versus texting? Do you think it makes a difference which method you use?

3. What are the benefits of placing a phone call instead of sending a text or an email?

LOOK IN THE WORD:

1. Read James 3:1-12. Explain some of the uses of the tongue.

2. Based on this verse, what message can you learn that can be applied to making phone calls or communicating face to face in relationships?

APPLICATION:

1. Remember the phone is a tool that can be used to help with communication with your loved ones.

2. Use your phone to send a positive text with encouraging words or simply say, "I love you" to those who have a special place in your heart.

JOURNAL:

Write about the power of a phone call. Imagine if the phone did not exist.

PHOTOS

DEFINITION: Photograph; to take pictures.

DISCUSSION QUESTIONS:

1. Do you enjoy taking pictures? Why or why not?

   _____
   _____
   _____

2. How do you think taking pictures can be a blessing in a marriage?

   _____
   _____
   _____

3. Do you have any photos from your childhood?

   _____
   _____
   _____

LOOK IN THE WORD:

1. Philippians 4:8 says whatever things are true, whatever things are noble, whatever things are just, whatever things are pure, whatever things are lovely, whatever things are of good report, if there ... meditate on these things.

   _____
   _____
   _____

2. How can taking pictures of various events, special days and happy times help you to apply this scripture?

   _____
   _____
   _____

APPLICATION:

1. Take pictures frequently, especially for special occasions.
2. Store your pictures in a place where you and others will always be able to enjoy them.
3. If you have children, be sure to take plenty of pictures as they grow so quickly.
4. Travel with your camera.
5. Create memories. Your pictures will often outlive you.

EXTRA ACTIVITY:

Get a photo book or some photos and discuss the memories that you have. If you do not have a photo book, create one. Take some pictures, get them developed and start creating some photo memories.

JOURNAL:

Someone once said, "A picture is worth a thousand words." Find a picture and write words to describe what is going on in the picture. Use details.

PRAYER

DEFINITION: Communication with God.

DISCUSSION QUESTIONS:

1. What is prayer? Why is it necessary?

2. Do you have a prayer partner?

3. How can prayer be an effective tool in your single life?

4. How do you currently go about handling challenges, disagreement or struggles in your life?

LOOK IN THE WORD:

1. Read Matthew 18:20. How can this verse be applied to your life?

2. What are the benefits of two people praying together?

APPLICATION:

1. Start your day with prayer. Remember Matthew 6:33.

2. Pray for your friends, family, neighbors, co-workers and your potential spouse.

3. Have an ongoing conversation with God throughout the day.

4. As you pray, be sure to praise God, give thanks, repent of any wrongdoing, make your request known and be committed to coming to God.

JOURNAL:

Write a prayer unto the Lord. Pour out your heart and concerns to the Lord.

CHAPTER SEVENTEEN
THE Q PRINCIPLES

QUARRELS

DEFINITION: An angry dispute. A disagreement marked by a temporary or permanent break in relations.

DISCUSSION QUESTIONS:

1. How do you normally handle disagreements with family or close friends?

2. What are your usual feelings/actions after having a disagreement with family or a close friend?

3. Do you remember seeing how your parents handled disagreements? Have you learned any lessons from seeing how your parents handled disagreements?

LOOK IN THE WORD:

1. Read II Timothy 2:23-24. What does this scripture say about having quarrels?

2. How can you apply this to your relationships with family and friends?

3. How would God have you to handle your disagreements?

APPLICATION:

1. It's okay to disagree but be sure to disagree without physical abuse.
2. Realize that you don't have to agree on everything. This is where you have to agree to disagree.
3. If necessary, wait until things are calm, and then talk about your feelings.
4. Discuss your feelings in a timely fashion; don't allow the anger to build and don't hold it in for a long time.
5. It is okay to get angry, but it is what you do with your anger that makes the difference.
6. Learn to take your concerns, frustrations, and disappointments to God in prayer. He is the only One who has the power to make a change.

JOURNAL:

Do you think God is pleased with the way that you handle your disagreements? Write a prayer to the Lord. If necessary, ask Him to forgive you for anything that may have offended Him or someone else.

_____
_____
_____
_____
_____
_____
_____
_____
_____
_____
_____
_____
_____
_____
_____
_____

QUEEN

DEFINITION: The wife of a king.

DISCUSSION QUESTIONS:

1. What does being treated like a queen mean to you?
   _____
   _____
   _____

2. The author mentions having a royal mentality toward others. Is this something that you have? If not, would you be willing to embrace treating others like royalty?
   _____
   _____
   _____

3. List two things that you are currently doing to make others feel special (those close to you).
   _____
   _____
   _____

LOOK IN THE WORD:

1. Read I Peter 2:9. Fill in the blanks. But you are a _____ generation, a _____ priesthood, a _____ nation. His own _____ people that you may _____ the praises of Him who _____ you out of darkness into His _____ light.

2. God views us as royal and special. Can you view yourself and others as royalty?
   _____
   _____
   _____

APPLICATION:

1. Ask your close family member or friend if there is anything you can start doing to make them feel special.
2. Treasure the times you have with others. Tomorrow is not promised.
3. Embrace the royal mentality and treat others like royalty.

JOURNAL:

We are God's special people and He loves us so much. Reflect and write about God's royal mentality toward us.

QUIET

DEFINITION: Restrained in speech, manner, etc.

DISCUSSION QUESTIONS:

1. Review the *"Quiet" Principle* (page 80) and write what it means to have a quiet spirit.

   _____
   _____
   _____

2. Why do you think a quiet spirit is very precious in the sight of God?

   _____
   _____
   _____

3. Why do you think being quiet is so hard for many women?

   _____
   _____
   _____

LOOK IN THE WORD:

1. Read I Peter 3:4 and fill in the blanks . . . rather let it be the _____ person of the _____, with the incorruptible _____ of a _____ and _____ spirit.

2. Notice the words that are used to describe a gentle and quiet spirit. "Incorruptible beauty." What does this mean to you? Why does the Bible say that we can be cursed?

   _____
   _____
   _____

APPLICATION:

1. Pray before responding.
2. Make your point without raising your voice.
3. Respond in a way that pleases God.
4. Be mindful of your motives, the tone and the attitude in which you are speaking.

JOURNAL:

Examine yourself. What kind of spirit do you normally display? Is it gentle and quiet or more rough and noisy? Do you think that God is pleased? Why or why not?

QUIT

DEFINITION: To stop, cease or discontinue.

DISCUSSION QUESTIONS:

1. Have you ever had a day where you felt like quitting, but you didn't?

2. How did you move your thoughts from wanting to quit to persevering?

3. Compare quitting and persevering.

LOOK IN THE WORD:

1. Read I Corinthians 9:24-27. Think of your relationship with God (your waiting period) (pledge of purity/abstinence) as a race. What insights can you get from this passage?

2. What must you do to win in the race?

APPLICATION:

1. Don't quit! Hang in there.
2. If you feel like quitting, don't be ashamed to seek help.
3. Seek Godly counsel.
4. Read positive books. Apply what you learn.
5. Surround yourself with positive people and information that will encourage you.

JOURNAL:

"A quitter never wins and a winner never quits." What do you think about this statement? What does it mean to you?

CHAPTER EIGHTEEN
THE R PRINCIPLES

RECONCILIATION

DEFINITION: The act of reconciling, bringing something together again, restoring something back to its original condition.

DISCUSSION QUESTIONS:

1. Read the *Reconciliation Principle*. (page 83) What is the testimony that the author shares in this principle? What did God do?

2. God has the power to reconcile. Why do you think people do not take advantage of this power?

3. How can reconciliation help to save a family, children and loved ones?

LOOK IN THE WORD:

1. Read Matthew 5:23-25. What instructions are believers given in this passage?

2. If everyone practiced this principle, how would relationships be different?

APPLICATION:

1. Pray for reconciliation for your relationships, and those who are divorced or separated.
2. Believe God for reconciliation.
3. Focus on God's power, not on what anyone is saying or doing.
4. Discuss your desire to be reconciled with your family or friends.

JOURNAL:

As Christians, God wants us to have the "Ministry of Reconciliation." (II Corinthians 5:18) He forgives us and reconciles us, so what do you think God wants us to do for others?

RELATIONSHIPS

DEFINITION: A connection, association or involvement between people.

DISCUSSION QUESTIONS:

1. Read the *Relationship Principle* (page 84) What are some of the key ingredients to building relationships?

2. List the relationships that are most important to you.

3. Why is it important to make time for building relationships with friends and family?

4. What are you doing to maintain relationships with friends and family members?

LOOK IN THE WORD:

1. Read the Ten Commandments. (Exodus 20:1- 17) Notice how the sixth through the ninth commandments are about people, their lives, relationships and property. Is God concerned about relationships? How do we know?

2. What instructions can we get on relationships from the Ten Commandments?

APPLICATION:

1. Be intentional about spending time with family and friends.
2. Invite family and friends over so they can spend time with you and your potential spouse.
3. Make phone calls and send a text to keep the lines of communication open.
4. Don't be so caught up into your world that you don't take time for others.

JOURNAL:

Pray about your relationships with family and friends. What would God have you do to make the relationships better? How can you be a light for Jesus in each of those relationships?

RESPECT

DEFINITION: The condition of being highly esteemed or honored.

DISCUSSION QUESTIONS:

1. Ask your parents or any authority figures what makes them feel respected?

   _____
   _____
   _____

2. On a scale of 1-10 with 10 being the highest, how are you doing with respecting the authorities in your life? (rate yourself)

   _____
   _____
   _____

3. Ask your authority figure if he or she is pleased with the level of respect that you give? (accept their response without debate)

   _____
   _____
   _____

LOOK IN THE WORD:

1. Read Leviticus 19:3. What is the message that we can learn from this verse?

   _____
   _____
   _____

2. The word revere means to respect and to obey. Do you revere your parents?

   _____
   _____
   _____

APPLICATION:

1. Find out what makes your authority figures feel respected, and do it.
2. Be careful of the way that you talk to others. Watch your tone and attitude.
3. Do not argue in public. Save your disagreements for private settings.
4. Consider God and your authority figures when making decisions.

JOURNAL:

What is God saying to you about respect?

CHAPTER NINETEEN
THE S PRINCIPLES

SEASONS

DEFINITION: One of the four periods of the year; spring, summer, fall or winter.

DISCUSSION QUESTIONS:

1. What is your favorite season? Why?

2. Have you ever experienced something in your life that was so tough, you didn't know if you could endure?

3. What type of season are you in right now? Explain why you selected this season.

LOOK IN THE WORD:

1. Read Ecclesiastes 3:1-8. Based on the list in the Bible, list at least three seasons you have personally experienced.

2. What would you say is the key to making it through the various seasons of life?

APPLICATION:

1. When you are experiencing a rough season, spend more time in prayer, Bible reading and worship.
2. Praise God in the midst of every season.
3. Be careful of how you treat others in the midst of each season.
4. Don't make any fast decisions in the midst of the rough seasons. Wait on the Lord.

JOURNAL:

No matter what season you are in, God is there. He said that He will never leave you nor forsake you. Write a letter to God thanking Him for carrying you through the various seasons of your life.

_____
_____
_____
_____
_____
_____
_____
_____
_____
_____
_____
_____
_____
_____
_____

SERVING

DEFINITION: To render assistance, be of use or help.

DISCUSSION QUESTIONS:

1. Have you ever been in a restaurant where the server was attentive to all of your needs? How did it make you feel?

2. What are your favorite ways to be served? (e.g., laundry, manicure, pedicure, spa treatment, etc.)

3. Read the last paragraph of the *Serving Principle* (page 89). What does the author say about the best servants?

4. Do you agree? Why or why not?

LOOK IN THE WORD:

1. Read Matthew 20:28. What can we learn from Jesus's example?

2. How can this principle apply to relationships?

APPLICATION:

1. Express your appreciation for the services that you may currently receive from others.
2. Look for ways to serve others every day.
3. Make serving God a priority.
4. Look for opportunities to serve in your church, community, etc.

JOURNAL:

One of the most important things to check while serving is our attitude. Galatians 5:13 says serve one another in love. What does it mean to serve in love?

_____
_____
_____
_____
_____
_____
_____
_____
_____
_____
_____
_____
_____
_____
_____
_____
_____

SEX

DEFINITION: To engage in sexual intercourse.

DISCUSSION QUESTIONS:

1. What were some of the first lessons you remember being taught about sex? How do these lessons line up with the Word of God?

   _____
   _____
   _____

2. List two things you are doing to honor God with your body.

   _____
   _____
   _____

3. Why do you think God created sex for married people only?

   _____
   _____
   _____

LOOK IN THE WORD:

1. Read I Corinthians 7:5. What are the instructions given to married people?

   _____
   _____
   _____

2. Read Song of Solomon 2:7. What are the instructions given to the single daughters?

   _____
   _____
   _____

APPLICATION:

1. Make abstinence a part of your standard of living while you are single.
2. Find ways to combat sexual temptations.
3. Pray and depend on God for strength to remain pure during your season of singleness.
4. Get accountability!

JOURNAL:

Write a pledge to God about maintaining sexual purity as a single.

SUBMISSION

DEFINITION: To submit, to give over, yield to the power or authority of another.

DISCUSSION QUESTIONS:

1. What do you think about submission?

    _____
    _____
    _____

2. What could make submitting difficult?

    _____
    _____
    _____

3. Before submitting to each other, who is the first person that each should submit to?

    _____
    _____
    _____

4. How do you submit to God? Give an example.

    _____
    _____
    _____

LOOK IN THE WORD:

1. Read Ephesians 5:21-22. Fill in the blanks. Submitting to _____ _____ in the fear of _____. Wives submit to your own _____, as to the _____.

2. Why is it important to be submitted to God before anyone else?

    _____
    _____
    _____

APPLICATION:

1. Submit to God first through prayer, reading and obeying His word.
2. Submit to one another.
3. Don't marry a person that you are not willing to submit to.
4. Observe the lifestyle and decisions of a potential spouse before deciding to marry.
5. Pray about all decisions.

JOURNAL:

"Submitting to God first makes it easier to submit to each other." Write your thoughts about this statement.

CHAPTER TWENTY
THE T PRINCIPLES

TEMPTATION

DEFINITION: Tempting, enticing, inviting or allurement.

DISCUSSION QUESTIONS:

1. What tempts you in a relationship?

2. What triggers your temptation? (e.g., music, movie, social media, television, a man or a woman)

3. What plan of escape do you have?

4. What scripture can you apply to your temptation?

LOOK IN THE WORD:

1. Read Matthew 4:8-10. How was Jesus tempted?

2. How did Jesus deal with the temptation?

APPLICATION:

1. Spend regular time in God's Word.
2. Learn to identify God's way from Satan's way.
3. Establish accountability with a friend.
4. Memorize I Corinthians 10:13.

JOURNAL:

Write about a temptation that you yielded to. What were the consequences, and how could you have handled it differently?

TIME

DEFINITION: A limited period or interval.

DISCUSSION QUESTIONS:

1. What are the two basic categories of time that the author mentions in the *Time Principle*? (page 93)

2. Do you enjoy spending time alone or do you always feel like you need to be with someone?

3. What are some of the things that may hinder time alone or time with others?

LOOK IN THE WORD:

1. Read Mark 1:35. How does spending time with God help you?

2. What are the benefits of having time alone?

APPLICATION:

1. Plan regular time alone, with friends, and with family.
2. Pray about how you should spend your time each day.

JOURNAL:

What is God saying to you about your time?

TITHE

DEFINITION: One tenth of your earnings.

DISCUSSION QUESTIONS:

1. Do you tithe? Why or why not?

2. Why do you think people struggle with giving their tithes?

3. What are some of the benefits/blessings of tithing?

LOOK IN THE WORD:

1. Read Malachi 3:8-11. How can you rob God?

2. What are the consequences of robbing God?

APPLICATION:

1. Give at least 10% of all of your increase.
2. Give cheerfully.
3. Make tithing a priority.
4. Place tithing in your budget. Pay God first.

JOURNAL:

God loves a cheerful giver. What is your attitude toward giving? Is God pleased?

TRUST

DEFINITION: A person on whom on one relies; a thing on which one relies.

DISCUSSION QUESTIONS:

1. Have you ever placed your trust in someone and felt disappointed because they let you down?

2. Where or whom should your trust be placed?

3. What are the benefits of putting your trust in the Lord?

LOOK IN THE WORD:

1. Read Psalm 40:4. What does this verse say about trust?

2. Have you been putting your trust in the Lord?

APPLICATION:

1. Read God's Word and His promises.
2. Trust God for everything that you need.
3. Remember, God will never leave you nor forsake you.

JOURNAL:

I am reminded of a song that says "I Will Trust in the Lord." Are you willing to fully trust the Lord? What does "trust the Lord" mean to you?

_____

_____

_____

_____

_____

_____

_____

_____

_____

_____

_____

_____

_____

_____

_____

CHAPTER TWENTY-ONE
THE U PRINCIPLES

UNDERSTANDING

DEFINITION: Knowledge of or familiarity with a particular thing.

DISCUSSION QUESTIONS:

1. What is the *Understanding Principle* (page 99) about?

2. Do you feel that you understand yourself?

3. Why do you think the scripture (I Peter 3:7) asks the husbands to dwell with understanding?

4. How can having an understanding of yourself reduce conflict in a relationship?

LOOK IN THE WORD:

1. Read I Peter 3:7. Fill in the blanks. "Husbands, likewise, _____ with them with _____, giving _____ to the _____, as to the _____ vessel, and as being heirs _____ of the grace of life, that your _____ may not be _____. What is the husband being instructed to do?

2. Proverbs 9:10 says that the fear of the Lord is the beginning of wisdom and knowledge of the Holy One is understanding. What does this verse tell you about understanding?

APPLICATION:

1. Spend time getting to know yourself better. Knowing yourself allows you to be comfortable with who you are.

2. Make an effort to understand your friends, family or potential spouse.

3. Reflect on your upbringing, life as a child, family experiences and things learned as a child. Reflection on these things can sometimes help us to understand who we are and why we do the things that we do.

JOURNAL:

Have you ever been misunderstood? How did it feel? Explain why, with God, we never have to worry about being misunderstood.

UNGODLY

DEFINITION: Sinful, wicked, not accepting God or His principles.

DISCUSSION QUESTIONS:

1. What is the focus of the *Ungodly Principle*? (page 99)

   _____
   _____
   _____

2. Do you have a sincere desire to please the Lord?

   _____
   _____
   _____

3. How can you develop a life that is pleasing to the Lord?

   _____
   _____
   _____

4. What are some examples of ungodly practices from which you should separate yourself?

LOOK IN THE WORD:

1. I Thessalonians 5:22 says; "Abstain from every form of evil." Are there forms of evil that you have allowed into your life, consciously or unconsciously?

   _____
   _____
   _____

2. How can ungodly habits become toxic to relationships?

APPLICATION:

1. Pray and examine your life thoroughly -- work habits, finances, thought patterns, and spiritual practices. See if there is anything that is ungodly that may be hindering your walk with the Lord.
2. In everything that you do, strive to please God.
3. Study the Word of God so you will be more knowledgeable and sensitive to the will of God.

JOURNAL:

Godly versus ungodly; compare and contrast a godly single life versus an ungodly single life. What are the differences?

_____
_____
_____
_____
_____
_____
_____
_____
_____
_____
_____
_____
_____
_____
_____
_____
_____
_____

UNITY

DEFINITION: The state of being one, united; oneness.

DISCUSSION QUESTIONS:

1. Do you feel that you live a life that is consistent with God's will? Why or why not?

2. What are some of your challenges with maintaining unity in your single life?

3. Why is it important to be on one accord with God's will for your life?

LOOK IN THE WORD:

1. Read Psalms 133:1. Based on this verse, what are the benefits of dwelling together in unity?

2. What can you do to help promote unity/oneness in your own life?

APPLICATION:

1. Seek God about your goals and plans.
2. Pray with close friends regularly for you and your potential spouse.
3. Have a discussion about your short-term and long-term goals with your potential spouse.

JOURNAL:

"Where the spirit of unity dwells, that's where you find the Lord." What does this statement mean to you?

UPLIFT

DEFINITION: To lift up, raise, elevate.

DISCUSSION QUESTIONS:

1. Have you ever been down and had someone to come along to say something that uplifted you?

2. Can your friends and family count on you to be uplifting?

3. What current situations are weighing you down?

4. Name two things that help to uplift your spirit.

LOOK IN THE WORD:

1. Read I Peter 5:7. What instructions does this verse give?

2. Read Ecclesiastes 4:9 and fill in the blanks.
   Two are _____ than one, because they have a good _____ for their labor. For if they _____, one will _____ up his companion.

APPLICATION:

1. Read the Word of God on a daily basis. God's Word alone is uplifting.
2. Listen to music that will uplift your soul.
3. Speak words of life not death.
4. Read positive books that will encourage you on your journey.
5. Stick post-its with affirming quotes around your home and work spaces.

JOURNAL:

"Love lifted me, Love lifted me, when nothing else could help, Love lifted me." How can the lyrics of this old song give instructions on uplifting each other? What is the key ingredient?

CHAPTER TWENTY-TWO
THE V PRINCIPLES

VACATION

DEFINITION: A period of suspension or freedom from work, duty or other activity.

DISCUSSION QUESTIONS:

1. Based on the *Vacation Principle* (page 103), what effect can a vacation have on a marriage relationship?

2. What is your idea of a perfect vacation?

3. When was the last time you had a vacation? How did you feel after the vacation?

LOOK IN THE WORD:

1. Read Genesis 2:2. What did God do on the seventh day?

2. If God took time to rest from ALL of His work, shouldn't we?

APPLICATION:

1. If possible, plan a getaway for you and friends/family.
2. If going away for any length of time is not possible, try taking a day trip.
3. Be sure to give yourself mini-vacations on the weekend. This helps to refuel your body for the week.
4. Practice mental vacations where you separate your mind from stress and to-do lists.
5. Be intentional about having days where you rest from ALL work.

JOURNAL:

If you could go on a vacation anywhere in the world, where would you go? (Pretend that time, money and childcare are not issues.)

_____
_____
_____
_____
_____
_____
_____
_____
_____
_____
_____
_____
_____
_____

VALIDATE

DEFINITION: To make valid, confirm or give approval.

DISCUSSION QUESTIONS:

1. Have you ever noticed when a husband is speaking next to his wife, people often look at the wife's face for validation (and vice versa)?

   _____
   _____
   _____

2. Did you know your friends may be looking for you to validate some of the decisions that they have made?

   _____
   _____
   _____

3. Do you validate your friends when they are talking in public? If not, explain.

   _____
   _____
   _____

LOOK IN THE WORD:

1. Read Numbers 30:10-16. This passage is about women who made vows when they were single and when they got married they had to state whether or not they would still be able to keep their vows. The husband's responsibility was to validate his wife's vow or to overrule the vow. If he said nothing, the wife could keep her vows but if he spoke out, this meant that the wife's vows were not valid.

   _____
   _____
   _____

2. What can we learn from this passage?

   _____
   _____
   _____

APPLICATION:

1. Practice giving friends your full attention when they are speaking.
2. Discuss issues with friends privately.
3. Avoid embarrassing others publicly.
4. Speak positively about your friends and family in public.
5. Pray regularly about how you use your tongue.

JOURNAL:

Why is it important to validate our loved ones? Imagine the issues that could occur from not validating them.

VARIETY

DEFINITION: The state of being varied or different.

DISCUSSION QUESTIONS:

1. Have you ever heard the saying, "Variety is the spice of life?" What does this statement mean to you?

2. Which way do you prefer your food -- with seasoning or without? Explain why.

3. Are you willing to do something different for yourself or with friends this week? Write down two ideas.

4. How do you normally feel after you have tried something new and enjoyed it?

LOOK IN THE WORD:

1. Throughout the Bible, spices are referred to as something special, precious or pleasant. (Read the following references: Song of Solomon 5:13, Isaiah 59:2, II Chronicles 32:27)

2. How might adding variety -- "the spice of life" -- provide something special in your life?

APPLICATION:

1. Have a meal at a different restaurant.
2. Wear something different the next time that you meet with friends or family.
3. Try a different genre of movies or music.
4. Invite some friends to your home or arrange a get-together with friends.

JOURNAL:

"Variety really is the spice of life!" Write your thoughts about this statement.

VOWS

DEFINITION: A solemn promise, pledge or personal commitment.

DISCUSSION QUESTIONS:

1. Discuss the world's view of marriage vows.

   _____
   _____
   _____

2. How is the world's view of marriage different from God's view?

   _____
   _____
   _____

3. Why do you think so many couples give up on their marriage without considering their vows?

   _____
   _____
   _____

LOOK IN THE WORD:

1. Read Deuteronomy 23:21. Fill in the blanks. "When you make a _____ to the _____ your _____ , you shall not _____ to pay it; for the _____ your _____ will _____ require it of _____, and it would be _____ to you.

2. What does this verse tell us about vows?

   _____
   _____
   _____

APPLICATION:

1. Write a vow to the Lord!

2. Examine the vows you've made to the Lord in all areas of your life.

3. If necessary, share your vow with a good friend and ask them to hold you accountable.

JOURNAL:

What are some of the vows that God has made to His people?

CHAPTER TWENTY-THREE
THE W PRINCIPLES

WAIT

DEFINITION: To postpone or delay in expectation.

DISCUSSION QUESTIONS:

1. Can you identify with the *Wait Principle*? (page 107) Explain.

2. What is your attitude in the midst of waiting?

3. Are you waiting on God to do something in you, your life, or in your situation?

LOOK IN THE WORD:

1. Read Lamentations 3:25-26. What does this scripture tell us about those who wait?

2. What should we be doing while we are waiting on the Lord to make a change in our lives?

APPLICATION:

1. Realize that you and your friends are different and your spouse will be different; therefore, it may be necessary to wait for them to change or for you to accept their ways.
2. Discuss your differences without getting angry.
3. Pray about the changes you would like to see in your private and professional life.
4. Wait on the Lord, with expectation, to make the change.
5. Remember, the Lord is the only one who can make a change in us or in our relationships. Wait patiently!

JOURNAL:

Why do you think God wants us to wait quietly? Explain how one can wait and not be quiet.

_____
_____
_____
_____
_____
_____
_____
_____
_____
_____
_____
_____
_____
_____
_____
_____

WEDDING RING

DEFINITION: A ring usually of precious metal given to the bride/groom during a wedding ceremony.

DISCUSSION QUESTIONS:

1. Read the *Wedding Ring Principle*. (page 108) What does the wedding ring symbolize?

2. Imagine driving without any signs (street signs, names of streets, stop signs, etc.). What do you think would happen?

3. How is a married person without a wedding ring similar to driving without having street signs?

4. How can a single person respect a person wearing a wedding ring?

LOOK IN THE WORD:

1. Read Esther 8:8. What was the purpose of the King's ring?

2. What is the purpose of a wedding ring? Why is it important for married people to wear a wedding ring?

APPLICATION:

1. As a single person, don't date anyone who is already wearing a wedding ring.
2. Honor the institution of marriage.
3. Remember that the wedding ring is an outward sign of a marriage covenant.
4. When you get married, always wear your ring.

JOURNAL:

Wedding rings are usually made of a precious metal like gold or silver. They are round with a never-ending circle. How is the wedding ring a good symbol of how God intended for marriage to be?

WITHHOLD

DEFINITION: To hold back or refrain from giving.

DISCUSSION QUESTIONS:

1. Review the *Withhold Principle*. (page 109) Have you ever experienced someone withholding something from you? How did it feel?

2. Can you think of something that you are withholding from the Lord, yourself, or close friends? If so, what are your reasons for withholding?

3. In your opinion, should married couples withhold good from each other?

LOOK IN THE WORD:

1. Proverbs 3:27 says; "Do not withhold good from those to whom it is due, when it is in the power of your hand to do so." What does this scripture mean to you?

2. Think about it. Is there anything within your power that you have not done?

APPLICATION:

1. If there is anything good (love, affection or kindness) that you have been withholding from someone you care about, give it to them.
2. If you feel that someone is withholding something from you, pray about it. Trust God to work it out!
3. Be willing to discuss your feelings with that person, but be patient if they still decide to withhold.
4. Try to get to the root of the problem. There is usually a reason for withholding.

JOURNAL:

Psalm 84:11 says; "For the Lord God is a sun and shield; The Lord will give grace and glory; No good thing will He withhold from those who walk uprightly." How does this verse bring comfort?

_____
_____
_____
_____
_____
_____
_____
_____
_____
_____
_____
_____
_____
_____
_____

WORDS

DEFINITION: Speech, talk or conversation.

DISCUSSION QUESTIONS:

1. Think about what you have been saying over the past week. What kind of words have you been speaking to yourself and others?

2. How do you feel when someone speaks words of encouragement to you?

3. Read the *Words Principle*. (page 110) What does it mean to bridle your tongue?

4. Have you ever said something and wished that you could take the words back? What did you do?

LOOK IN THE WORD:

1. Read Matthew 12:36. What does this verse tell us about our words?

2. Since we will give account for all of our words, how should we be speaking?

APPLICATION:

1. Remember that words hurt! Be selective about the words you speak.
2. Speak words that build up, encourage and help strengthen your relationships.
3. When you want to tell someone off, pray first and ask God to calm your spirit.
4. Find ways to give sincere compliments to your friends, family or co-workers.

JOURNAL:

"Sticks and stones may break my bones but words will never hurt me." What is wrong with this statement?

WORRY

DEFINITION: To torment oneself with or suffer from disturbing thoughts.

DISCUSSION QUESTIONS:

1. Have you ever spent time worrying?

2. Have you ever worried about the following; your future, your finances, your potential spouse or your children?

3. What are usually the effects of worrying?

LOOK IN THE WORD:

1. Read Matthew 6:25-34. What does God's word say about worrying?

2. Read Matthew 6:33. Instead of worrying what should we do?

APPLICATION:

1. Remember to cast all of your cares on the Lord for He cares for you.
2. Journal your thoughts and concerns. Trust God.
3. Keep your mind on the Lord in the midst of everything.
4. Discuss your worries with close friends and pray about them.

JOURNAL:

I remember some words in a song that said, "If you are going to pray then don't worry. If you are going to worry then don't pray." What do these words mean to you?

CHAPTER TWENTY-FOUR
THE X, Y, AND Z PRINCIPLES

X-RAY

DEFINITION: To examine.

DISCUSSION QUESTIONS:

1. Read the *X-Ray Principle*. (page 113) Explain the principle in your own words.

2. Have you ever seen an x-ray before? How is an x-ray similar to the *X-ray Principle*?

3. Have you ever wondered why you do some of the things that you do?

4. If you were to examine your own life's x-rays, what might you see?

LOOK IN THE WORD:

1. Read Lamentations 3:40-42. List three things that verse 40 instructs us to do.

2. These verses present a plan for repentance and renewal. Why might this be helpful to do before one gets married?

APPLICATION:

1. Examine yourself and think about the things you have experienced.
2. Repent for any sins God reveals to you.
3. Is there anything that may have happened long ago but is still causing issues for you today?
4. Seek the Lord. Allow him to clean you from the inside out.
5. Pray earnestly!

JOURNAL:

Having an x-ray is something that everyone needs to do. What are the benefits of having an x-ray and why would it be most helpful before one gets married?

_____
_____
_____
_____
_____
_____
_____
_____
_____
_____
_____
_____
_____
_____
_____

YOU

DEFINITION: One, anyone or people in general.

DISCUSSION QUESTIONS:

1. Have you ever prayed and asked God to "fix" something or someone?

2. What do you do when it seems like God isn't answering your prayer request?

3. Are you waiting for a change to take place?

4. What do you do while you are waiting for God to do something in your relationship with your potential spouse, your relationship with a loved one or in a professional relationship?

LOOK IN THE WORD:

1. Romans 12:2 says "Be transformed by the renewing of your mind." So if we want a change to take place, where should it start?

2. How can having a renewed mind help you?

APPLICATION:

1. Draw closer to God through prayer and reading His word.
2. Focus on you and what God wants you to do.
3. Be mindful of your conduct while you are waiting on God to make a change.
4. Ask God to help you to be loving and kind to your loved ones in the midst of waiting on a change.
5. Remember that change comes by renewing your mind.

JOURNAL:

"When you would like to see a change in your family or potential spouse, remember that change starts with you." Write your thoughts about this statement.

___
___
___
___
___
___
___
___
___
___
___
___
___
___

ZEBRA

DEFINITION: A horse-like African mammal with a characteristic pattern of black or dark-brown stripes on a whitish background.

DISCUSSION QUESTIONS:

1. Read the *Zebra Principle*. (page 115) What does a zebra and marriage have in common?

   _____
   _____
   _____

2. "Every marriage has its own black stripes and white stripes." What does this mean?

   _____
   _____
   _____

3. Have you experienced some black stripes and white stripes? Explain.

   _____
   _____
   _____

4. Have you ever looked at someone's marriage and thought, "I hope my marriage will be just like that?"

   _____
   _____
   _____

LOOK IN THE WORD:

1. Read I Thessalonians 5:18 and Romans 8:28. Write your thoughts about these verses.

   _____
   _____
   _____

2. How can you relate this verse to the *Zebra Principle*?

   _____
   _____
   _____

APPLICATION:

1. Thank God for your black stripes (bad days) and the white stripes (good days).
2. Draw closer to God through prayer and reading when you experience black stripes.
3. Don't compare your relationship to someone else's relationship.
4. Don't compare your potential spouse to someone else's spouse.

JOURNAL:

Marriage is like a zebra because _____. Complete this statement.

PERSONAL REFLECTIONS

1. Which principle or principles do you remember the most? Explain why.

   _____
   _____
   _____

2. Which principle presents the greatest challenge to you?

   _____
   _____
   _____

3. Think about the basic instructions that are given over and over throughout the book. (Pray, read your Bible and draw closer to God) How are you doing with following these instructions?

   _____
   _____
   _____

4. How might applying these principles benefit your life?

   _____
   _____
   _____

5. Do you know anyone else who can benefit from reading this book? If so, share it.

   _____
   _____
   _____

REFERENCES

Dictionary.com

The Holy Bible, New King James Version

www.ingramcontent.com/pod-product-compliance
Lightning Source LLC
Chambersburg PA
CBHW081355290426
44110CB00018B/2388